Phys~~ical Characteristics~~ of the
Irish Setter
(from The Kennel Club breed standard)

COLOUR
Rich chestnut with no trace of black. White on chest, throat, chin or toes or small star on forehead or narrow streak or blaze on nose or face not to disqualify.

COAT
On head, front of legs and tips of ears, short and fine, on all other parts of body and legs of moderate length, flat and as free as possible from curl or wave. All feathering to be as straight and flat as possible.

TOPLINE
Firm and straight, gently sloping downwards from the withers.

TAIL
Of moderate length proportionate to size of body, set on just below the level of the back, strong at root tapering to a fine point and carried as nearly as possible on a level with or below the back.

HINDQUARTERS
Wide and powerful.

RIBS
Well sprung leaving plenty of lung room and carried well back to muscular loin, slightly arched.

HINDLEGS
From hip to hock long and muscular, from hock to heel short and strong. Stifle and hock joints well bent and not inclined either in or out.

FEET
Small, very firm; toes strong, close together and arched.

Irish Setter

by Margaret Williams

Table of Contents

9

21

33

38

65

PUBLISHED IN THE
UNITED KINGDOM BY:

INTERPET
P U B L I S H I N G

Vincent Lane, Dorking
Surrey RH4 3YX
England

ISBN 1-902389-30-1

82

PHOTO CREDITS

Norvia Behling
TJ Calhoun
Carolina Biological Supply
Kent & Donna Dannen
Doskocil
Isabelle Francais
James Hayden-Yoav
James R Hayden, RBP
Carol Ann Johnson
Bill Jonas

Alice van Kempen
Dwight R Kuhn
Dr Dennis Kunkel
Mikki Pet Products
Antonio Philippe
Phototake
Jean Claude Revy
Dr Andrew Spielman
Karen Taylor
Michael Trafford
C James Webb

Illustrations by Renée Low

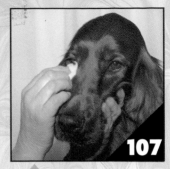

107

Housebreaking and Training Your Irish Setter
by Charlotte Schwartz
Be informed about the importance of training your Irish Setter from the basics of housebreaking, and understanding the development of a young dog, to executing obedience commands (sit, stay, down, etc.).

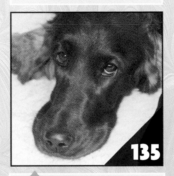

135

Health Care of Your Irish Setter
Discover how to select a proper veterinary surgeon and care for your dog at all stages of life. Topics include vaccination scheduling, skin problems, dealing with external and internal parasites and the medical conditions common to the breed.

Your Senior Irish Setter
Recognise the signs of an ageing dog, both behavioural and medical; implement a senior-care programme with your veterinary surgeon and become comfortable with making the final decisions and arrangements for your senior Irish Setter.

142

Showing Your Irish Setter
Experience the dog show world, including different types of shows and the making up of a champion. Go beyond the conformation ring to field trials, working trials and agility trials, etc.

Copyright © 2000 Animalia, Ltd.
Cover patent pending. Printed in Korea.

The Irish Setter has been named Supreme Champion of Crufts Dog Show three times in the 1990s. Here's the third victor, Sh Ch Caspians Intrepid, owned by Jackie Lorrimer and bred by Mr M and Mrs S Oakley. This prestigious win took place in 1999.

HISTORY OF THE
IRISH SETTER

The Irish Setter has been termed an artist's dream. In the world of dog art, they are considered to be the most beautiful of all dogs. With their brilliant red coat, long velvety ears and regal carriage, they command attention wherever they appear. Blessed with typical Irish charm and joviality, the Irish Setter captures the heart and imagination of everyone who sees or meets this dashing rogue.

Despite its regal bearing, the Irish Setter personality is affectionate, playful and full of mischief. Independent, highly intelligent and most anxious to please, this is a superb family companion who can prance around the show ring and still hunt admirably in the field.

Like many other hunting dogs, the Irish Setter is an ancient breed. Although Irish folklore offers many theories on its ancestry, history records that most setter breeds evolved from spaniel-type dogs that had their origins in Spain and were so named after that country. Breed historians find references to an Irish Spaniel in *The Laws of*

All canines evolved from the wolf, regardless of their breed or usage. Compare the above skeleton of an American wolf to the lower skeleton of a retriever and the similarities are self-evident.

Howell, an ancient tome written before the 11th century. The first mention of a 'setter' in literature appears in the 1570 work *De Canibus Britannicis*, revised in 1576. Author Dr Johannes Caius discusses different types of dogs and makes the first reference to a 'setter' as a dog that remains 'sure and silent' upon finding birds, then 'layeth his belly to the grounde and so creepeth forward like a worme.' Dr Caius's description is validated in the 1616 publication *The Country Farmer* where writers Surflet and Markham describe 'another sort of land spannyels which are called setters.'

Dogs of that long ago era were used in tandem with hawks or nets to capture birds. The dog would first search for game and, upon finding the birds, flush them into the air. The hunter then released his hawk, which would capture the bird, kill it and return it to the hunter.

The netting dogs were trained with more control. Once the dog had scented game, he would poise with foreleg raised and 'set,' pointing to indicate the location of the birds. On command he would drop to his belly and crawl closer to the game, where the hunter would then throw his net over both dog and bird.

Breeding habits of that time were planned according to the talents of the dog rather than any particular breed or variety. It is believed that in the 17th century, spaniels were crossed at times with Spanish Pointers, no doubt another part of Irish Setter

Once the preferred setter of Ireland, the Irish Red and White Setter is a direct relation to the more common Irish Setter. The two breeds are similar in conformation except coloration.

ancestry, and by the 18th century 'setter' dogs were recognised. In the 1804 tome *The Shooting Directory*, written by R B Thornhill, the Irish are credited with a Red and White Setter which was espoused by European sportsmen: 'There is no country in Europe that can boast of finer Setters than Ireland.'

It is also thought that the Irish Red Setter and the Irish Red and White Setter coexisted throughout Ireland during the early 1700s. Another theory suggests that a cross with the Irish Red Spaniel (or its Gaelic name, the *Mudder Rhu*) made up the Irish Setter.

Dr Caius, however, would have us believe otherwise. He notes that, 'The most part of their skynnes are white, and if they are marked with any spottes, they are commonly red, and somewhat

great therewithal,' which seems to indicate that selective breeding from white-and-red to predominantly red-and-white was already afoot in the 16th century.

Red Setter lines can be found in Irish history as far back as 1770. Maurice Nugent O'Connor was a devotee of the solid-red setter, although he also continued to breed the Red and White Setter as well. During the 1830s, Sir

George Gore established a large kennel of self-reds. Crossbreedings with the Gordon Setter, known then as the Black and Tan Setter, occasionally produced black markings or solid blacks, which were not tolerated, although slight white markings were acceptable. Even today a few black hairs on

The setter breeds all derived from similar hunting dog stock. Today's Irish Setter, along with the English and Gordon Setters, share like conformation, hunting style, and handsome appearances. Illustration by Lilian Cheviot.

DID YOU KNOW?

Although the Irish Red Setter was popular during the 1890s, The Kennel Club registered a scant 289 in 1891, and by the First World War, registrations had dropped to 25. Post-war registrations climbed to over 300 by 1921, and Irish Red Setter ranks swelled to over 2000 by the 1930s.

These two English Setters show off their distinctive blue belton coloration, a colour pattern unique to the English Setter breed.

A young Irish Setter exhibiting a quality head around 1900. This dog is Ch Carrig Maid, owned by Mrs M Ingle Bepler.

an Irish Red Setter are a disqualification in the show ring.

The prominent dog authority and author J W Walsh (who wrote under the pseudonym Stonehenge) wrote, 'The blood red or rich chestnut or mahogany colour is the colour of the Irish Setter of high mark. This colour must be unmixed with black; studied in a strong light, there must not be black shadows or waves, much less black fringes to the ears, or to the profile of the form.' Walsh's comments lend credence to the occasionally disputed theory about crossbreedings to the Gordon Setter in Irish Setter origins.

During the 1800s, several prominent Irish families developed their own strains of setters, and many kept detailed breeding records. The Marquis of Waterford, Lords Dillon and Clancarty, Sir George Gore, the Earls of Lismore and others took great pride in their own lines of Irish Setters. By the late 1800s, self-red setters dominated the dog

The modern Gordon Setter, once simply called the Black and Tan Setter for its distinctive coat colour, is an elegant, substantially built hunting dog, of course closely related to the Irish Setter.

scene over the red-and-whites, and it became apparent that such selective breeding was for pure colour. Although the Irish Setter was still used primarily as a working gundog, the beauty of this handsome and imposing red dog gave breeders and owners an excuse to show their gundogs on the bench.

In 1859 the first dog show in England was held at Newcastle-upon-Tyne with entries limited to only setters and pointers. Breeders quickly became enamoured with these canine beauty pageants and the opportunity to display their lovely dogs. As yet there was no accepted standard for any breed, thus there were major differences in breed type and appearance. It would be a quarter century before

Ch Clancarty Rhu was a Red Setter from the early 1900s owned by Mrs M Ingle Bepler. Note the differences in the head type between Rhu and Maid.

a standard for the breed was conceived for breeders and exhibitors.

The first Irish Red Setter to distinguish the breed as a show star was a dog named Bob, owned by Major Hutchinson, who claimed a first prize at an all-

This handsome dog owned by Mrs F C Hignett is Ch Bryan O'Lynn, photographed in the early 1900s.

breed event held in Birmingham, England in 1860. There was much disagreement at the time about what made up the ideal Irish Red Setter. As the first Irish Setter show dog of importance, Bob was the undisputed stud dog of the day, and his impact was felt for many generations after his time on the bench. He was the grandsire of the very famous field dog, Plunket, bred by the Reverend Robert O'Callaghan and owned by the Reverend J Cumming Macdona, who was one of the founders of The Kennel Club in 1873. Plunket was also a brother to a dog called Rover, used by Stonehenge in his book *Dogs in the British Islands* as an illustration of the ideal Irish Setter. Rover's dam was Macdona's Grouse, a daughter of Bob, evidence that Bob left an important dual imprint on breed quality at that time.

Plunket was also successful in the show ring and was later purchased by Mr R L Purcel Llewellin for 100 guineas. Llewellin is best known for having created the famous strain of Llewellin field trial English Setters, and some wonder if Plunket was partially responsible for the quality of those dogs. Llewellin later sold Plunket for export to America for a then-unheard-of price of 100 pounds.

Another very important show dog, Ch Palmerston, was owned by Mr Cecil Moore of Omagh, County Tyrone, who was an advocate of the working gundog. Although Palmerston lacked the stamina and physical properties required for substantial field work, his physical attributes made him a natural for a show career. Legend has it that Mr Moore was about to drown Palmerston because of his lack of field potential, when his friend T M Hilliard begged to take the dog and show him on the bench. Mr Moore agreed and Palmerston's new career was launched.

Palmerston was a lean and narrow dog with a long, narrow head, unlike most other setters of that time who carried the thicker spaniel skull and foreface. Despite his age of five years, he set records as a show dog and was widely used at stud. His long, lean look, together with the famous white stripe that marked his forehead, soon became the hallmark of the breed and was known as the 'Palmerston stripe.' When Palmerston died in 1880, Hilliard's son was the manager of the world-famous Waldorf Astoria Hotel in New York City. Hilliard arranged to have Palmerston's head mounted and placed on display at the hotel where it remained until 1918 when it was donated to the Irish Setter Club of America.

The year 1882 witnessed the formation of the Irish Red Setter

These two red beauties are engaged in a game of chase. Like all hunting dogs, the Irish Setter has a fair amount of energy to burn daily.

Club. On 29 March 1886, members approved a standard for the Irish Red Setter based on a scale of points for the head, body, coat and feathering. Although that point scale was dropped in later years, the standard underwent some minor change and is still observed today.

Despite the new popularity of showing in the ring, breeders still wanted to test the working ability of their dogs in competition. The Irish Setter already had proven itself to be a worthy hunter and most obedient in the field, although many sportsmen still contended the breed was wilful and stubborn and that the dark red coat was hard to see in the field.

The first field trial was held in 1865. The first Irish Setter to win at such an event was the Reverend Macdona's Plunket who, at two years old, won a second place at the Shrewsbury Trials in May 1870. After Plunket's export to the United States, he became a most popular sire. His American progeny were of superb quality and excelled in the field as well as on the bench.

As with most other breeds of dogs, the working Irish Red Setter suffered a decline in popularity due to the First World War. Several prominent show kennels,

1886 SCALE OF POINTS FOR THE IRISH RED SETTER:

Head: 10 points
Eyes: 6 points
Ears: 4 points
Neck: 4 points
Body: 20 points
Hind Legs and Feet: 10 points
Fore Legs and Feet: 10 points
Tail: 4 points
Coat and Feather: 10 points
Colour: 8 points
Size, Style, General Appearance: 14 points

however, were able to prevail and become influential within the breed during the early 1900s.

The Rheola Kennel, owned by Mrs Ingle Ball Bepler, was founded in the early 1890s prior to her marriage. Her three foundation bitches were out of the highly influential stud dog, Ch Palmerston, who can be found generations back in almost every Irish Setter pedigree.

Mrs Bepler's breedings produced several important show dogs, including Clancarty Rhu, the sire of Ch Rheola Toby who was a twice grandsire of the important Sh Ch Rheola Bryn. Bryn was bred twice to Rheola Mallie, and the two produced many winners and top producers during their time. Unfortunately those breedings are also thought to have contributed to the spread of the progressive

retinal atrophy (PRA) gene in the Irish Setter breed. This is a fairly widespread congenital disease of the eyes.

Possibly Mrs Bepler's most important dog was Ch Norna, out of Ch Rheola Didona by Loc Garmain Barney, who during her career won a total of 18 Challenge Certificates (CCs) and reigned as the top brood bitch for 40 years, having also produced 7 CC winners.

In the late 1920s, Mrs Bepler wrote a book on her chosen breed, which contains names and photographs of at least eight generations of her own breedings, from 1898 until Ch Rheola Bryndona in 1928. In her writings she offered her theories about the three colour varieties in the breed, stating that the self-red prevailed in Northern Ireland, the red and white dominated the west and south of Ireland, and the speckled

Whether or not your Irish Setter will be trained to compete in field trials, your dog will welcome the opportunity to romp in the field for exercise and fellowship.

DID YOU KNOW?

During the Second World War, large-breed dogs suffered a serious decline in numbers. Breeders were unable to feed their dogs, and in many cases they had their dogs euthanised rather than watch their beloved dogs starve to death.

Irish Setters that derive from quality breeders will have strong hips and excellent eyes. Regardless of an owner's intention for his Irish Setter, it is essential that the dog be able to act and play like a dog.

variety featuring white spots (sometimes called 'shower of hail') were indigenous to the western coast of Ireland.

A fierce competitor, Mrs Bepler was determined to succeed with her line of Irish Setters. In 1908, together with several other breed fanciers, she broke ranks with the Dublin Irish Red Setter Club and formed the Irish Setter Association, England, and was appointed as club secretary. This new organisation aimed itself directly at native Irish breeders, and limited membership privileges to residents of England, Wales and Scotland.

The first Irish Setter to reach the epitome of stardom was Judd's Ch Strabane Sally, who won the Gundog Group in 1908 at the prestigious Crufts Show. By the 1930s, the gorgeous chestnut Irish Red Setter was firmly established as a breed, almost unchallenged in beauty in the canine world.

The next breed winner was Tuite's Ch Astley's Portia of Rua, already a Field Trial Champion, who not only took the Gundog Group in 1981 but also became the first Irish Setter to claim the ultimate, Best in Show. Two years

DID YOU KNOW?
Author Anna Redlich's book *The Dogs of Ireland* tells a very remarkable tale of an Irish Setter skeleton discovered still 'on point' over one year after his owner had lost him in a bog.

later Levick's Sh Ch Corriecas Fergus won the Group and went on to take Reserve Best in Show.

It speaks well of Irish Setter breed excellence, showmanship and beauty that during the 1990s three more Irish Setters earned the top award at Crufts. In 1993 Jackie Lorrimer's Sh Ch Danaway Debonair was given the honour under judge Tom Horner. Again in 1995 Rachel Shaw's Sh Ch Starchelle Chicago Bear went on to Best in Show under M George Down. Finally, in 1999 Sh Ch Caspians Intrepid won this top award for owner Jackie Jorrimer and breeder Mr M and Mrs S Oakley.

As with all breeds that experience a surge of success, the Irish Setter developed health problems during its rise in popularity. During the 1930s, PRA began to appear in several prominent lines of Irish Setters.

As more and more dogs became affected, PRA was widely debated over the next ten years. By 1940 it had been determined that PRA was indeed hereditary and would lead to partial and eventually total blindness. Further research into the pedigrees of affected dogs established that many of Mrs Bepler's Rheola dogs were carriers of the PRA gene, and due to their wide use in popular breeding programmes, many bloodlines were affected. It was a sad fact that even blind animals were still being bred in an attempt to produce a winning dog. Fortunately, nothing like this even be fathomed in the dog world today.

By 1945 the problem had reached such proportions that The Kennel Club issued a ruling that no Irish Setter could be registered or transferred without a signed statement declaring neither parents nor grandparents were actively affected with the disease, and that the dog in question had not produced a case of PRA.

Mr Rasbridge, as secretary of the Irish Setter Association, then devised a plan requiring test matings to identify carriers and clear animals. Such a design was obviously not popular with the important breeders of that decade. As affected pups were identified, the breed was

Opposite page: Fortunate for the Irish Setter, dedicated breeders banned together to eradicate existing health issues that plagued the breed during popularity surges. Today's Irish Setters are sound of mind and body.

DID YOU KNOW?

During the 1800s, controversy raged over the advantages and disadvantages of hunting over a solid red dog. Feeling prevailed that the self-reds would fade into the surrounding cover and run the danger of being shot. Some who preferred and bred self-reds would tie a white scarf around their dogs' necks to make them stand out against the field.

devastated with many champions, and other famous Irish Setters retired after their test matings failed. In what may be the most energetic attempt to salvage any breed, conscientious Irish Setter breeders continued to test mate and clear their stock. The next ten years were spent rebuilding Irish Setter lines and kennels. Their efforts eventually produced several influential dogs that carried the breed back from the brink of genetic disaster.

CHARACTERISTICS OF THE
IRISH SETTER

In addition to his achievements in the show ring and afield, the Irish Setter is also a most appealing family companion. His boundless energy and enthusiasm for life are part of his irresistible Irish charm. Although his hunting heritage demands that he enjoy ample opportunity to run and exercise, he adapts well to family living as long as his owner provides enough space and activity to satisfy those needs. A postage-stamp size garden will not suffice, unless you are prepared for long daily walks in all types of weather. He cannot simply run free for exercise, as he will follow his hunting instincts and run off. It is also wise to remember that he was bred for the endurance to work in the field all day, and therefore will be a very hyperactive dog indoors if not provided outlets for his energy. You must give an Irish Setter plenty of exercise and a job to do to make him a happy dog. Training for field work, obedience or agility trials or the show ring will provide adequate outlets for the abundance of Irish Setter energy.

The Irish Setter companion dog relates well to every member of his family, regardless of his or her age, and his loyalty, especially to children, is absolute. Thus he can be protective and will rise to the occasion if he feels his family is threatened or in danger. He is not considered a good watchdog as he is not a barker and seldom vocalises. Although he is not aggressive, he will announce the approach of visitors, and his size alone might deter a home invader. He is not easily intimidated, nor does he feel the need to become hostile or aggressive with other dogs, regardless of their breed or size.

Irish Setters are slow to mature both mentally and physically, and they often seem to resist growing up at all, remaining clownish and puppy-like well into their veteran years. The breed is naturally clean and will housetrain quickly and easily if given the opportunity whilst still a youngster. They are very people-oriented and prefer to live with their human family members. If confined to kennel life or deprived of human companionship, they can easily become destructive and unmanageable.

Opposite page: The charms of the Irish Setter pup are irresistible. Breed members resist growing up, in mind and spirit, and will remain puppy-like for years to come.

21

OWNER QUALIFICATIONS

Not every dog lover is properly suited to live with an Irish Setter or provide him with the type of home or environment that he requires to lead a quality life. If he doesn't have what he needs, the quality of human life also becomes questionable, since an unhappy Irish Setter will surely become disruptive and out of control. An owner must possess the patience and sense of humour necessary to enjoy this amiable breed to the fullest.

If you are contemplating a future with this breed, you should look deep into your dog-loving soul and ask yourself if you are willing to do the following:

• Live with constant high-energy activities for the next ten years.

• Have the patience and endurance to accept, and yes, enjoy the trials and tribulations of living with a grown-up puppy for four or five years.

• Accept the responsibility for all future life changes, the dog's and your own, including such events as new babies, children in school, or moving to a new home.

• Give your Irish Setter at least two hours of attention and exercise each and every day.

• Train your Irish Setter to become a well-behaved family member who would be welcome anywhere in your community.

• Provide proper veterinary care, including annual check-ups, vaccinations, spay or neuter, and emergency health care. Can you afford it and are you willing to spend the money?

• Keep your Irish Setter safe at all times, whether in the house, garden or car, never chain him outside or permit him to ride loose in an open truck.

• Become educated about the proper care of this breed, correct training methods and good grooming habits.

• Consult your breeder or other dog professional if you have questions or concerns before they become real problems.

The Irish Setter's affectionate temperament and outgoing personality make him a wonderful choice for young and old alike.

• Accept full responsibility for the dog's well being regardless of his age, infirmity, future disability or health problem.

• Take whatever time necessary to find a responsible breeder and select the right puppy for your family.

If you can answer 'Yes' to every question, you are ready to begin life as an Irish Setter human companion. Start your puppy search early, as most good breeders often have a waiting list. Don't rush into a pup and don't become discouraged by a wait. The right puppy is always worth waiting for!

ACTIVITIES FOR THE IRISH SETTER

The Irish Setter is often considered the reigning monarch of the show ring. His regal bearing, elegant head, imposing structure and gleaming chestnut coat create instant electricity in the show ring. His beauty and commanding presence create an aura that enthrals both judge and spectator. It is no small surprise that a dog so beautiful would progress from field work to dominate the show scene.

SHOWING YOUR IRISH SETTER

In Britain, all dog shows are held under the auspices of The Kennel Club and run according to their rules and licensing regulations. Several types of informal show events are frequently hosted by

As lovely and ornamental as the Irish Setter can be in your home, the breed needs considerable exercise. An active Irish Setter is a happy home companion.

the various canine groups to allow exhibitors to acclimate their young hopefuls to the show scene and to introduce newcomers to the world of show dogs.

The Challenge Certificates (CC) necessary to make up a Show Champion may be earned only at Championship Shows. A CC is awarded to each Best of Sex winner at shows where CCs are offered. A dog must win three CCs under three different judges in order to earn the Show Champion (Sh Ch) title. If he accomplishes this feat before he is one year old, he must win another CC after that time before the title is awarded. As a slow-maturing breed, few Irish Setters become Show Champions in this manner.

To become a full Champion (Ch) in the breed, an Irish Setter must also prove his ability in the field by earning a Certificate of Merit (CM) or placement at a field trial, or by gaining a Show Gundog Working Certificate in a field test.

Many young people enjoy training their dogs and participating with them in various types of competition.

To become an Irish Show Champion in his native land, an Irish Setter must earn 40 Green Star points, including four Majors of at least five points each. Points are determined by the number of dogs entered in the show. An Irish Champion title requires a field qualification as well.

There is much more to showing and winning with a dog than trotting about the ring with your lovely dog at the end of a show lead. The dog's physical fitness and attributes, his coat condition, proper grooming and gaiting as well as handler composure and attire all contribute to success in the show ring. Irish Setter owners interested

in bench competition should align themselves with other show fanciers to acquaint themselves with the rules and finer points of this canine activity.

FIELD TRIALS
The title of Field Champion (FT Ch) is the most difficult of titles, and few Irish Setters today achieve this lofty status. A dog must win two first prizes in the Open Stake under two different judges at two different field trial competitions for Setters and Pointers, or win the separate Setter and Pointer Championship Stake.

Few Irish Setters today compete seriously in the field. As

showing in conformation attracts more and more breeders to the show ring, the breed continues to falter as a dependable working gun dog. The Irish Setter has emerged as a sometimes happy-go-lucky clown who is excitable and wilful with a strong tendency to be hyperactive. Of the gundog breeds, they are considered the most difficult to train. Indeed they are affectionate and eager to please, but they often display a headstrong attitude in the field, and training is a lengthy, demanding, and often frustrating task. Because they are by nature sensitive, slow to mature and somewhat stubborn, training requires a kind but firm demeanour, a great deal of patience, and a thorough understanding of the breed's natural abilities and tendencies. Most experienced trainers warn that too much pressure at an early age can 'burn out' even the most talented of dogs. If you hope to train your Irish Setter for any kind of field activity, it would be important to find an experienced person to advise you and to study several good books on the subject before joining a training group.

OTHER ACTIVITIES

The very enthusiastic Irish Setter is a natural for the high-energy and challenging sport of agility. Specta-

Puppies should not be rushed into competitive pursuits. Given the chance to settle down and grow into their substantial frames, young Irish Setters can excel in many different arenas, including showing, agility and field trials.

the Irish Setter is discussed in more detail later, the new owner should be aware of some hereditary conditions in the breed. This is not meant to alarm a new owner or dissuade a potential owner from the breed; rather, just to raise awareness so that owners will be educated and able to choose a healthy, well-bred pup and give it the best possible care throughout its life.

Properly educated owners understand the requirements of stimulating their Irish Setters and will acquire their dogs only from reputable breeders who screen their progeny for potential hereditary illnesses.

tors thrill to watch the athletic Irish Setter joyously zooming through the agility course obstacles with typical Irish grace and glee.

However, the Irish Setter is less successful in obedience competition. Although he enjoys working with his person, he bores easily and may create his own obedience routine, amusing to the gallery, but stressful and unpredictable for the owner or handler of the dog.

Beyond competition events, the breed's gentle and affectionate disposition has opened up a new career as therapist to residents of nursing homes, schools, hospitals and rehabilitation centres. Irish Setters display an amazing ability to understand the needs of every patient, and observers say the dogs thoroughly enjoy their visits. Many Irish Setters participate in PAT programmes to the delight of many needy residents and patients.

HEALTH CONCERNS

Although general health care for

PROGRESSIVE RETINAL ATROPHY (PRA)

PRA is an hereditary degenerative disease that will eventually lead

to blindness. It is passed to progeny through a simple autosomal recessive gene, which means that both the sire and dam must be carriers for their offspring to become affected.

An owner wishing to certify his dog as free from PRA must be referred to a referee by the examining veterinarian. The referee will examine the dog and review the veterinarian transfer certificate as well as the dog's Kennel Club registration certificate. The referee signs his report, gives one copy to the owner, sends a copy to the British Veteri-

nary Association (BVA), and keeps one copy for himself. If the report is favourable, The Kennel Club will then issue a permanent or interim certificate of clearance.

Today this disease also can be identified through DNA testing, which is available at the Animal Health Trust. Your veterinarian can draw a small blood sample to be forwarded for testing.

HIP DYSPLASIA (HD)

Hip dysplasia simply means poor or abnormal development of the hip joint where the ball and socket do not function properly. It is common in most large breeds of dogs and is considered to be an inherited disorder. To diagnose HD, your veterinarian will x-ray your dog and submit those films to the BVA and The Kennel Club for evaluation. A severe case of HD can render a working dog worthless in the field or other activities, and even a mild case can cause painful arthritis in the average house dog.

Whilst hip dysplasia is a largely inherited condition, research shows that environmental factors play a significant role in its development. Overfeeding and feeding a diet high in calories (primarily fat) during a large-breed puppy's rapid-growth stages are suspected to be contributing factors in the development of HD. Heavy-bodied and overweight puppies are more at risk than pups with very lean conformation.

Irish Setter puppies that derive from quality stock will be cleared for potential eye and hip problems. Eyes can be checked as early as six to eight weeks, although hips cannot be cleared until two years of age.

27

The BVA has joined with The Kennel Club to help curb the incidence of hip dysplasia in all breeds of dogs. Irish Setters over one year of age and under six years of age should be x-rayed by a veterinary surgeon. The x-rays are submitted to a special board of veterinarians who specialise in reading orthopaedic films. If the dog shows no evidence of abnormality, a certificate of clearance is issued by The Kennel Club. To correctly identify the dog under evaluation, The Kennel Club requires the dog's date of birth and Kennel Club registration number to be recorded on the x-ray. The purpose of such screening is to eliminate affected dogs from breeding programmes, with the long-term goal of reducing the incidence of HD in the affected breeds.

Irish Setters that show marked evidence of hip dysplasia should never be bred. Anyone looking for a healthy Irish Setter pup should make certain the sire and dam of any litter under consideration have their certificates of clearance.

BLOAT (GASTRIC DILATATION/ VOLVULUS)

Bloat is a life-threatening condition that is most commonly seen in very deep-chested breeds such as the Irish Setter, Weimaraner, Great Dane, Boxer and several other similarly constructed breeds. It occurs when the stomach fills up rapidly with air and begins to twist,

DO YOU KNOW ABOUT HIP DYSPLASIA?

Hip dysplasia is a fairly common condition found in purebred dogs. When a dog has hip dysplasia, its hind leg has an incorrectly formed hip joint. By constant use of the hip joint, it becomes more and more loose, wears abnormally and may become arthritic.

Hip dysplasia can only be confirmed with an x-ray, but certain symptoms may indicate a problem. Your dog may have a hip dysplasia problem if it walks in a peculiar manner, hops instead of smoothly runs, uses his hind legs in unison (to keep the pressure off the weak joint), has trouble getting up from a prone position or always sits with both legs together on one side of its body.

As the dog matures, it may adapt well to life with a bad hip, but in a few years the arthritis develops and many dogs with hip dysplasia become cripples.

Hip dysplasia is considered an inherited disease and can usually be diagnosed when the dog is three to nine months old. Some experts claim that a special diet might help your puppy outgrow the bad hip, but the usual treatments are surgical. The removal of the pectineus muscle, the removal of the round part of the femur, reconstructing the pelvis and replacing the hip with an artificial one are all surgical interventions that are expensive, but they are usually very successful. Follow the advice of your veterinary surgeon.

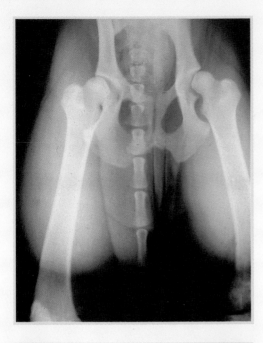

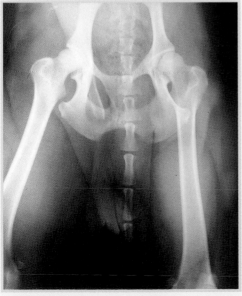

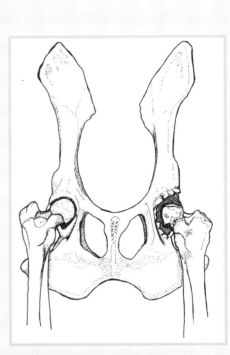

The illustration above shows a healthy hip joint on the left and an unhealthy hip joint on the right. Hip dysplasia can only be positively diagnosed by x-ray, Irish Setters manifest the problem when they are between four and nine months of age, the so-called fast-growth period.

Compare x-rays of the the two hip joints on the left and you'll understand dysplasia better. Hip dysplasia is a badly worn hip joint caused by improper fit of the bone into the socket. It is easily the most common hip problem in Irish Setters.

cutting off the blood supply. If not treated immediately, the dog will go into shock and die.

The development of bloat is sudden and unexplainable. The dog will become restless and his stomach will appear swollen or distended, and he will have difficulty breathing. The dog must receive veterinary attention at once in order to survive. The vet must relieve the pressure in the stomach and surgically return the stomach to its normal position. Research has confirmed that the structure of the Irish Setter contributes to his predisposition to this condition. Nevertheless, there are several precautions you can take to reduce the risk:

• Feed your dog twice daily rather than offer one large meal.

• Do not exercise your dog for at least an hour before and two hours after eating.

• Make sure your dog is calm and not overly excited whilst he's eating. It has been shown that nervous or overly excited dogs who gulp or wolf their food are more prone to develop bloat.

• Add a small portion of moist meat product to his dried food ration.

• Do not permit the dog to have water with his meals. It's advisable to refrain from offering water one hour before and after each meal.

CANINE LEUCOCYTE ADHESION PROTEIN DEFICIENCY (CLAPD) OR CANINE GRANULOCYTOPATHY (CGS)

This is an inherited immune disorder that affects a dog's ability to combat bacterial infection and is thought to be specific to the Irish Setter. Affected puppies are unable to ward off infections from superficial wounds or lesions and are extremely vulnerable to respiratory infections and complications. At about 10 to 14 weeks of age, pups may develop gingivitis (inflammation of the gums) or inflammation of the joints, especially at the jaws or knees. They will run an elevated temperature and be unable to eat or stand up. Antibiotics provide only a temporary respite, as puppies will relapse as soon as medication is discontinued. The prognosis is very poor for affected animals, and most are humanely euthanised.

Fortunately a test has been developed to diagnose this disorder. Research is currently underway to provide DNA testing to identify carriers of CLAPD and CGS.

EPILEPSY

Epilepsy is a seizure disorder caused by abnormal electrical patterns in the brain. It affects almost all breeds and even mixed breeds, although the Irish Setter, amongst other breeds, appears to have inherited a predisposition to this disorder.

Primary epilepsy, also known as idiopathic, genetic, inherited, or true epilepsy, is difficult to diagnose, and there is no specific test for the disease. Diagnosis is generally drawn by ruling out other possibilities. Primary epilepsy usually occurs between the ages of six months and five years of age.

Secondary epilepsy refers to seizures caused by viral or infectious disease, metabolic disorders, chemical or nutritional imbalance or traumatic injury. Seizures are also associated with hypothyroidism, which is an inherited autoimmune disease common to many purebred dogs.

Although epilepsy is difficult to diagnose, dogs suffering recurring seizures, especially from an early age, are questionable breeding candidates.

MEGA-OESOPHAGUS (MO)

This is a condition that causes the oesophagus to become enlarged. Affected puppies are unable to retain milk or food and will regurgi-tate through the mouth or nose. They may cough excessively and make gurgling or rattling sounds. Difficult to diagnose in very young whelps, suspected cases can be confirmed through barium x-ray. Mild cases of MO may go unnoticed for many months. MO is thought to be inherited and should be researched before breeding.

THE IRISH SETTER RESCUE SCHEME

It is a sad fact of Irish Setter life that people purchase puppies on a whim with no idea about what makes up an Irish Setter or how to raise it properly. Most often the dog runs riot in the household, and the family throws up its hands in complete despair. Rescued animals taken in by the Scheme often show signs of neglect and may have health problems, making it difficult to place the dog in a new home.

The Irish Setter Rescue Scheme was founded in 1970 when the Irish Setter Breeders Club agreed to re-home a number of young dogs who were abandoned by their owners. Although rescue numbers have decreased in recent years due to increased public awareness of the responsibilities of dog ownership, the need for Irish Setter Rescue unfortunately will remain for years to come.

If you are interested in assisting with Irish Setter Rescue, any local Irish Setter club will welcome your request for information.

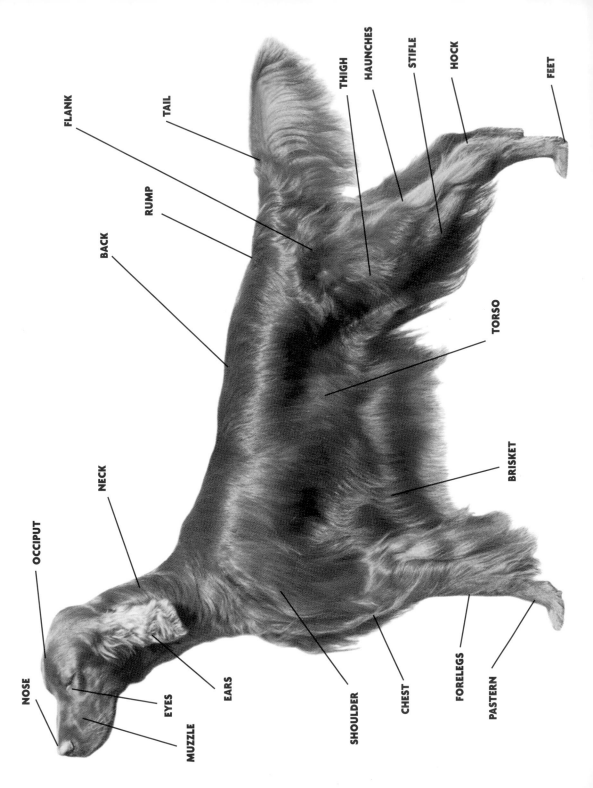

FLANK

TAIL

THIGH

HAUNCHES

STIFLE

HOCK

FEET

RUMP

BACK

TORSO

NECK

BRISKET

OCCIPUT

NOSE

EYES

EARS

MUZZLE

SHOULDER

CHEST

FORELEGS

PASTERN

All breeds need a standard. Without a specific profile or blueprint to follow, there would be no guidelines for breeders and within one or two generations, our dog of choice would look nothing like the breed we know and love.

The standard should be fully understood and subscribed to by anyone who cares about the Irish Setter. Only through generations of careful selection are we able to live with and enjoy the temperament and grand good looks of this regal breed of dog.

The most important characteristics of the Irish Setter are described in the first three paragraphs of the breed standard. His general appearance 'Must be racy, balanced and full of quality,' a description befitting a sporting dog with an elegant, symmetrical and flowing body. The word 'must' cannot be overlooked. His characteristics include 'tremendously active' and 'untiring,' qualities vital in a hunting dog, and not to be ignored or neglected when living as a family member. His temperament is 'demonstrably affectionate,' so essential for a quality family companion and tragically missing in some members of the breed today.

THE KENNEL CLUB BREED STANDARD FOR THE IRISH SETTER

General Appearance: Must be racy, balanced and full of quality. In conformation, proportionate.

Characteristics: Most handsome, and refined in looks, tremendously active with untiring readiness to range and hunt under any circumstances.

Temperament: Demonstrably affectionate.

The appearance of the Irish Setter must be 'racy, balanced and full of quality.' Dogs at shows are compared to the breed standard to determine their strengths and weaknesses.

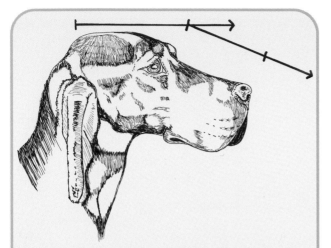

Faulty head, snipy; head and muzzle not parallel; pendulous flews.

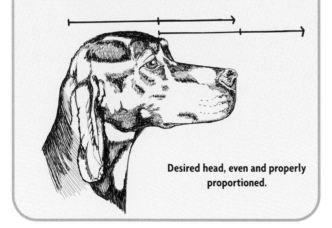

Desired head, even and properly proportioned.

square at end. Jaws of nearly equal length, flews not pendulous, nostrils wide. Colour of nose dark mahogany, dark walnut or black.

Eyes: Dark hazel to dark brown, not too large, preferably like an unshelled almond in shape, set level (not obliquely), under brows showing kind, intelligent expression.

Ears: Of moderate size, fine in texture, set on low, well back and hanging in a neat fold close to head.

Mouth: Jaws strong, with a perfect, regular and complete scissor bite, i.e. upper teeth closely overlapping the lower teeth and set square to the jaws.

Neck: Moderately long, very muscular but not too thick, slightly arched and free from all tendency to throatiness, setting cleanly without a break of topline into shoulders.

Forequarters: Shoulders fine at points, deep and sloping well back. Forelegs straight and sinewy having plenty of bone, with elbows free, well let down and not inclined either in or out.

Body: Chest as deep as possible, rather narrow in front. Ribs well sprung leaving plenty of lung room and carried well back to

Head and Skull: Head long and lean, not narrow or snipy, not coarse at the ears. Skull oval (from ear to ear) having plenty of brain room and well-defined occipital protuberance. From occiput to stop and from stop to tip of nose to be parallel and of equal length, brows raised showing stop. Muzzle moderately deep, fairly

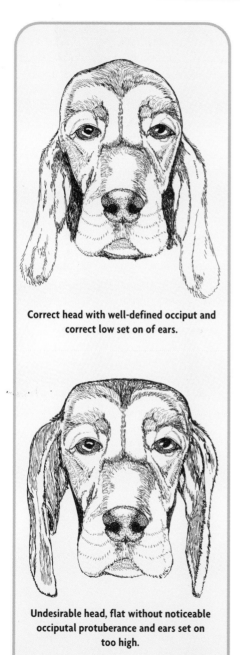

Correct head with well-defined occiput and correct low set on of ears.

Undesirable head, flat without noticeable occiputal protuberance and ears set on too high.

muscular loin, slightly arched. Firm straight topline gently sloping downwards from the withers.

Hindquarters: Wide and powerful. Hindlegs from hip to hock long and muscular, from hock to heel short and strong. Stifle and hock joints well bent and not inclined either in or out.

Feet: Small, very firm; toes strong, close together and arched.

A popular choice for showing, the Irish Setter is a top contender at conformation shows. Because the breed is handsome and highly trainable, it has earned many top awards at dog shows, including winning the show of shows, Crufts Dog Show.

35

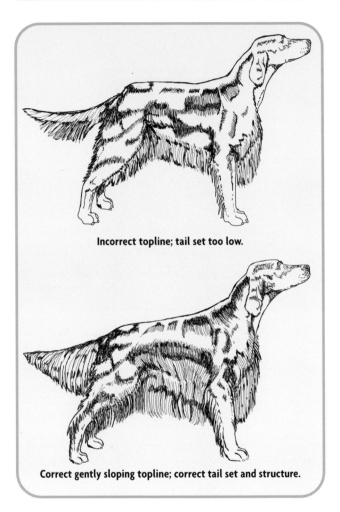

Incorrect topline; tail set too low.

Correct gently sloping topline; correct tail set and structure.

rear, and in profile, showing perfect co-ordination.

Coat: On head, front of legs and tips of ears, short and fine, on all other parts of body and legs of moderate length, flat and as free as possible from curl or wave. Feathers on upper portion of ears long and silky; on back of fore- and hindlegs long and fine. Fair amount of hair on belly, forming a nice fringe which may extend on to chest and throat. Feet well feathered between toes. Tail to have fringe of moderately long hair decreasing in length as it approaches point. All feathering to be as straight and flat as possible.

Colour: Rich chestnut with no trace of black. White on chest, throat, chin or toes or small star on forehead or narrow streak or blaze on nose or face not to disqualify.

Tail: Of moderate length proportionate to size of body, set on just below the level of the back, strong at root tapering to a fine point and carried as nearly as possible on a level with or below the back.

Gait/Movement: Free flowing, driving movement with true action when viewed from front or

FAULTS:
Any departure from the foregoing points should be considered a fault and the seriousness with which the fault should be regarded should be in exact proportion to its degree.

NOTE:
Male animals should have two apparently normal testicles fully descended into the scrotum.

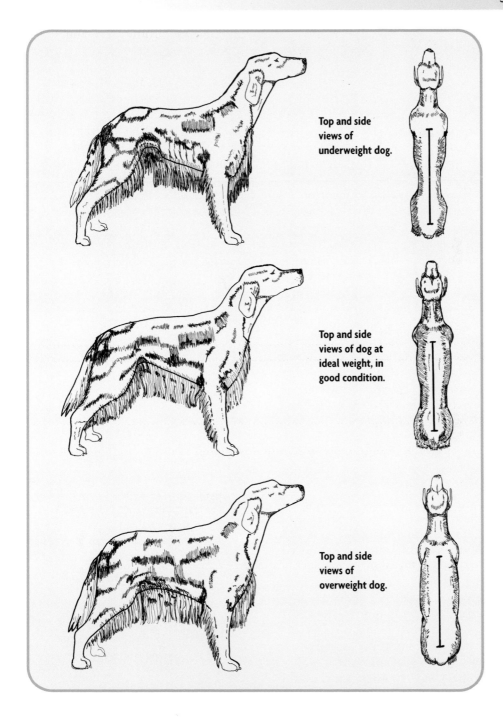

Top and side
views of
underweight dog.

Top and side
views of dog at
ideal weight, in
good condition.

Top and side
views of
overweight dog.

IRISH SETTER

WHERE TO BEGIN?

If you are convinced that the Irish Setter is the ideal dog for you, it's time to learn about where to find a puppy and what to look for. Locating a litter of Irish Setters should not present a problem for the new owner. You should enquire about breeders in your area who enjoy a good reputation in the breed. You are looking for an established breeder with outstanding dog ethics and a strong commitment to the breed. New owners should have as many questions as they have doubts. An established breeder is indeed the one to answer your four million questions and make you comfortable with your choice of the Irish Setter. An established breeder will sell you a puppy at a fair price if, and only if, the breeder determines that you are a suitable, worthy owner of his/her dogs. An established breeder can be relied upon for advice, no matter what time of day or night. A reputable breeder will accept a puppy back, without questions, should you decide that this not the right dog for you.

When choosing a breeder, reputation is much more important than convenience of location. Do not be overly impressed by breeders who run brag advertisements in the presses about their stupendous champions and working lines. The real quality breeders are quiet

> **DID YOU KNOW?**
>
> Unfortunately, when a puppy is bought by someone who does not take into consideration the time and attention that dog ownership requires, it is the puppy who suffers when he is either abandoned or placed in a shelter by a frustrated owner. So all of the 'homework' you do in preparation for your pup's arrival will benefit you both. The more informed you are, the more you will know what to expect and the better equipped you will be to handle the ups and downs of raising a puppy. Hopefully, everyone in the household is willing to do his part in raising and caring for the pup. The anticipation of owning a dog often brings a lot of promises from excited family members: 'I will walk him every day,' 'I will feed him,' 'I will housebreak him,' etc., but these things take time and effort, and promises can easily be forgotten once the novelty of the new pet has worn off.

DID YOU KNOW?
You should not even think about buying a puppy that looks sick, undernourished, overly frightened or nervous. Sometimes a timid puppy will warm up to you after a 30-minute 'let's-get-acquainted' session.

and unassuming. You hear about them at the dog trials and shows, by word of mouth. You may be well advised to avoid the novice who lives only a couple miles away. The local novice breeder, trying so hard to get rid of that first litter of puppies, is more than accommodating and anxious to sell you one. That breeder will charge you as much as any established breeder. The novice breeder isn't going to interrogate you and your family about your intentions with the puppy, the environment and training you can provide, etc. That breeder will be nowhere to be found when your poorly bred, badly adjusted four-pawed monster starts to growl and spit up at midnight or eat the family cat!

Whilst health considerations in the Irish Setter are not nearly as daunting as in some other breeds, socialisation is a breeder concern of immense importance. Since the Irish Setter's temperament can vary somewhat from line to line, socialisation is the

first and best way to encourage a proper, stable personality.

Choosing a breeder is an important first step in dog ownership. Fortunately, the majority of Irish Setter breeders are devoted to the breed and its well being. New owners should have little problem finding a

DID YOU KNOW?
Your puppy should have a well-fed appearance but not a distended abdomen, which may indicate worms or incorrect feeding, or both. The body should be firm, with a solid feel. The skin of the abdomen should be pale pink and clean, without signs of scratching or rash. Check the hind legs to make certain that dewclaws were removed, if any were present at birth.

Visiting a dog show proves most helpful in meeting top-quality breeders from whom you can acquire your Irish Setter puppy. Never approach a handler when he or she is busy preparing or showing their dog. Wait until the judging is finished.

DID YOU KNOW?
Your selection of a good puppy can be determined by your needs. A show potential or a good pet? It is your choice. Every puppy, however, should be of good temperament. Although show-quality puppies are bred and raised with emphasis on physical conformation, responsible breeders strive for equally good temperament. Do not buy from a breeder who concentrates solely on physical beauty at the expense of personality.

needs, it's time to visit the litter. Keep in mind that many top breeders have waiting lists. Sometimes new owners have to wait as long as two years for a puppy. If you are really committed to the breeder whom you've selected, then you will wait (and hope for an early arrival!). If not, you may have to resort to your second or third

DID YOU KNOW?
Breeders rarely release puppies until they are eight to ten weeks of age. This is an acceptable age for most breeds of dog, excepting toy breeds, which are not released until around 12 weeks, given their petite sizes. If a breeder has a puppy that is 12 weeks or more, it is likely well socialised and housetrained. Be sure that it is otherwise healthy before deciding to take it home.

reputable breeder who doesn't live on the other side of the country (or in a different country). The Kennel Club is able to recommend breeders of quality Irish Setters, as can any local all-breed club or Irish Setter club. Potential owners are encouraged to attend field trials to see the Irish Setters in action, to meet the breeders and handlers firsthand and to get an idea what Irish Setters look like outside of a photographer's lens. Provided you approach the handlers when they are not terribly busy with the dogs, most are more than willing to answer questions, recommend breeders and give advice.

Now that you have contacted and met a breeder or two and made your choice about which breeder is best suited to your

It wouldn't be difficult to find a friendly, attractive puppy from this litter of Irish Setter puppies. Be sensible, not sentimental, in choosing your future companion.

choice breeder. Don't be too anxious, however. If the breeder doesn't have any waiting list, or any customers, there is probably a good reason. It's no different than visiting a pub with no clientele. The better pubs and restaurants always have a waiting list—and it's usually worth the wait. Besides, isn't a puppy more important than a pint?

Since you are likely choosing an Irish Setter as a pet dog and not a field dog, you simply should select a pup that is friendly and attractive. Irish Setter litters vary from one to twelve, so selection may be limited or great once you have located a desirable litter. While the basic structure of the breed has little variation, each puppy will have a unique person-ality. Beware of the shy or overly aggressive puppy: be especially conscious of the nervous Irish Setter pup. Don't let sentiment or emotion trap you into buying the runt of the litter.

INSURANCE
Many good breeders will offer you insurance with your new puppy, which is an excellent idea. The first few weeks of insurance will probably be covered free of charge or with only minimal cost, allowing you to take up the policy when this expires. If you own a pet dog, it is sensible to take out such a policy as veterinary fees can be high, although routine vaccinations and boosters are not covered. Look carefully at the many options open to you before deciding which suits you best.

If you have intentions of using your new charge for hunting, there are many more considera-tions. The parents of a future working dog should have excellent qualifications, including actual work experience as well as working titles in their pedigrees.

The gender of your puppy is largely a matter of personal taste, although there is a common belief amongst those who work with Irish Setters that bitches are quicker to learn and generally more loving and faithful. Males learn more slowly but retain the lesson longer. The difference in size is noticeable but slight.

Coloration of the pups varies from dark mahogany to light fawn. True adult colour does not emerge until the adolescent coat change.

Breeders commonly allow visitors to see the litter by around the fifth or sixth week, and puppies leave for their new homes between the eighth and tenth week. Breeders who permit their puppies to leave early are more interested in your pounds than their puppies' well being. Puppies need to learn the rules of the trade from their dams, and

ARE YOU A FIT OWNER?

If the breeder from whom you are buying a puppy asks you a lot of personal questions, do not be insulted. Such a breeder wants to be sure that you will be a fit provider for his puppy.

Puppies are the children of the dog world, and this quartet of growing toddlers are ready for play and socialisation. Nothing is easier in life than making friends with a puppy.

most dams continue teaching the pups manners and dos and don'ts until around the eighth week. Breeders spend significant amounts of time with the Irish Setter toddlers so that they are able to interact with the 'other species,' i.e. humans. Given the long history that dogs and humans have, bonding between the two species is natural but must be nurtured. A well-bred, well-socialised Irish Setter pup wants nothing more than to be near you and please you.

Always check the bite of your selected puppy to be sure that it is neither overshot or undershot. This may not be too noticeable on a young puppy but it is wise to check for overall soundness.

COMMITMENT OF OWNERSHIP
After considering all of these factors, you have most likely

DOCUMENTATION
Two important documents you will get from the breeder are the pup's pedigree and registration papers. The breeder should register the litter and each pup with The Kennel Club, and it is necessary for you to have the paperwork if you plan on showing or breeding in the future.

Make sure you know the breeder's intentions on which type of registration he will obtain for the pup. There are limited registrations which may prohibit the dog from being shown or from competing in non-conformation trials such as Working or Agility if the breeder feels that the pup is not of sufficient quality to do so. There is also a type of registration that will permit the dog in non-conformation competition only.

YOUR SCHEDULE . . .
If you lead an erratic, unpredictable life, with daily or weekly changes in your work requirements, consider the problems of owning a puppy. The new puppy has to be fed regularly, socialised (loved, petted, handled, introduced to other people) and, most importantly, allowed to visit outdoors for toilet training. As the dog gets older, it can be more tolerant of deviations in its feeding and toilet relief.

---

already made some very important decisions about selecting your puppy. You have chosen an Irish Setter, which means that you have decided which characteristics you want in a dog and what type of dog will best fit into your family and lifestyle. If you have selected a breeder, you have gone a step further—you have done your research and found a responsible, conscientious person who breeds quality Irish Setters and who should be a reliable source of help as you and your puppy adjust to life together. If you have observed a litter in action, you have obtained a firsthand look at the dynamics of a puppy 'pack' and, thus, you should learn about each

pup's individual personality—perhaps you have even found one that particularly appeals to you.

However, even if you have not yet found the Irish Setter puppy of your dreams, observing pups will help you learn to recognise certain behaviour and to

determine what a pup's behaviour indicates about his temperament. You will be able to pick out which pups are the leaders, which ones are less outgoing, which ones are confident, which ones are shy, playful, friendly, aggressive, etc. Equally as important, you will learn to recognise what a healthy pup should look and act like. All of these things will help you in your search, and when you find the Irish Setter that was meant for you, you will know it!

Researching your breed, selecting a responsible breeder and observing as many pups as possible are all important steps on the way to dog ownership. It may seem like a lot of effort...and you have not even brought the pup home yet! Remember, though, you cannot be too careful when it comes to deciding on the type of dog you want and finding out about your prospective pup's background. Buying a puppy is not—or should not be—just another whimsical purchase. This is one instance in which you actually do get to choose your own family! You may be thinking

DID YOU KNOW?

The cost of food must also be mentioned. All dogs need a good quality food with an adequate supply of protein to develop their bones and muscles properly. Most dogs are not picky eaters but unless fed properly they can quickly succumb to skin problems.

Litter socialisation is vital to the development of puppies' personalities. Observe how the littermates interact to understand the temperament of each pup.

that buying a puppy should be fun—it should not be so serious and so much work. Keep in mind that your puppy is not a cuddly stuffed toy or decorative lawn ornament, but a creature that will become a real member of your family. You will come to realise that, whilst buying a puppy is a pleasurable and exciting endeavour, it is not something to be taken lightly. Relax…the fun will start when the pup comes home!

Always keep in mind that a puppy is nothing more than a baby in a furry disguise…a baby who is virtually helpless in a human world and who trusts his owner for fulfilment of his basic needs for survival. In addition to water and shelter, your pup needs care, protection, guidance and love. If you are not prepared to commit to this, then you are not prepared to own a dog.

Wait a minute, you say. How hard could this be? All of my neighbours own dogs and they seem to be doing just fine. Why should I have to worry about all of this? Well, you should not worry about it; in fact, you will probably find that once your Irish Setter

DID YOU KNOW?
Taking your dog from the breeder to your home in a car can be a very uncomfortable experience for both of you. The puppy will have been taken from his warm, friendly, safe environment and brought into a strange new environment. An environment that moves! Be prepared for loose bowels, urination, crying, whining and even fear biting. With proper love and encouragement when you arrive home, the stress of the trip should quickly disappear.

45

pup gets used to his new home, he will fall into his place in the family quite naturally. But it never hurts to emphasise the commitment of dog ownership. With some time and patience, it is really not too difficult to raise a curious and exuberant Irish Setter pup to be a well-adjusted and well-mannered adult dog—a dog that could be your most loyal friend.

PREPARING PUPPY'S PLACE IN YOUR HOME

Researching your breed and finding a breeder are only two aspects of the 'homework' you will have to do before bringing your Irish Setter puppy home. You will also have to prepare your home and family for the new addition. Much as you would prepare a nursery for a newborn baby, you will need to designate a place in your home that will be the puppy's own. How you prepare your home will depend on how much freedom the dog will be allowed. Whatever you decide, you must ensure that he has a place that he can 'call his own.'

When you bring your new puppy into your home, you are bringing him into what will become his home as well. Obviously, you did not buy a puppy so that he could take over your house, but in order for a puppy to grow into a stable,

well-adjusted dog, he has to feel comfortable in his surroundings. Remember, he is leaving the warmth and security of his mother and littermates, as well as the familiarity of the only place he has ever known, so it is important to make his transition as easy as possible. By preparing a place in your home for the puppy, you are making him feel as welcome as possible in a strange new place. It should not take him long to get used to it, but the sudden shock of being transplanted is somewhat traumatic for a young pup. Imagine how a small child would feel in the same situation—that is how your puppy must be feeling. It is up to you to reassure him and to let him know, 'Little chap, you are going to like it here!'

WHAT YOU SHOULD BUY
CRATE

To someone unfamiliar with the use of crates in dog training, it may seem like punishment to shut a dog in a crate, but this is not the case at all. Although all breeders do not advocate crate training, more and more breeders and trainers are recommending crates as a preferred tool for pet puppies as well as show puppies. Crates are not cruel—crates have many humane and highly effective uses in dog care and training.

For example, crate training is a popular and very successful housebreaking method. A crate can keep your dog safe during travel; and, perhaps most importantly, a crate provides your dog with a place of his own in your home. It serves as a 'doggie bedroom' of sorts—your Irish Setter can curl up in his crate when he wants to sleep or when he just needs a break. Many dogs sleep in their crates overnight. When lined with soft bedding along with

Pet supply shops offer a variety of crates that are suitable for your Irish Setter.

PHOTO COURTESY OF DOSKOCIL.

CRATE TRAINING TIPS

During crate training, you should partition off the section of the crate in which the pup stays. If he is given too big an area, this will hinder your training efforts. Crate training is based on the fact that a dog does not like to soil his sleeping quarters, so it is ineffective to keep a pup in a crate that is so big that he can eliminate in one end and get far enough away from it to sleep. Also, you want to make the crate den-like for the pup. Blankets and a favourite toy will make the crate cosy for the small pup; as he grows, you may want to evict some of his 'roommates' to make more room.

It will take some coaxing at first, but be patient. Given some time to get used to it, your pup will adapt to his new home-within-a-home quite nicely.

his favourite toy, a crate becomes a cosy pseudo-den for your dog. Like his ancestors, he too will seek out the comfort and retreat of a den—you just happen to be providing him with something a little more luxurious than his early ancestors enjoyed.

As far as purchasing a crate, the type that you buy is up to you. It will most likely be one of the two most popular types: wire or fibreglass. There are advantages and disadvantages to each type. For example, a wire crate is more open, allowing the air to flow

through and affording the dog a view of what is going on around him whilst a fibreglass crate is sturdier. Both can double as travel crates, providing protection for the dog. The size of the crate is another thing to consider. Puppies do not stay puppies forever—in fact, sometimes it seems as if they grow right before your eyes. A small-sized crate may be fine for a very young Irish Setter pup, but it will not do him much good for long! Unless you have the money and the inclination to buy a new crate every time your pup has a growth spurt, it is better to get one that will accommodate your dog both as a pup and at full size. A large-size crate will be necessary for a full-grown Irish Setter, who stands approximately 27 inches high.

BEDDING

Veterinary bedding in the dog's crate will help the dog feel more at home and you may also like to pop in a small blanket. This will take the place of the leaves, twigs, etc., that the pup would use in the wild to make a den; the pup can make his own 'burrow' in the crate. Although your pup is far removed from his den-making ancestors, the denning instinct is still a part of his genetic makeup. Second, until you bring your pup home, he has been sleeping amidst the warmth of his mother and littermates, and whilst a blanket is not the same as a warm breathing body, it still provides heat and something with which to snuggle. You will want to wash your pup's bedding frequently in case he has an accident in his crate, and replace or remove any blanket that becomes ragged and starts to fall apart.

TOYS

Toys are a must for dogs of all ages, especially for curious

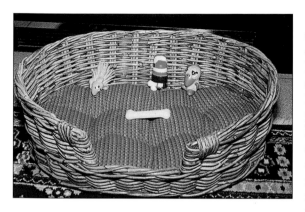

In addition to a crate, your Irish Setter will welcome a bed situated in the family room so that he can feel that he has a place close to his loved ones.

Irish Setter puppies are fairly aggressive chewers and only the hardest, strongest toys should be offered to them. Breeders advise owners to resist stuffed toys, because they can become de-stuffed in no time. The overly excited pup may ingest the stuffing, which is neither digestible nor nutritious.

Similarly, squeaky toys are quite popular, but must be avoided for the Irish Setter. Perhaps a squeaky toy can be used as an aid in training, but not for free play. If a pup 'disembowels' one of these, the small plastic squeaker inside can be dangerous if swallowed. Monitor the condition of all your pup's toys carefully and get rid of any that have been chewed to the point of becoming potentially dangerous.

Be careful of natural bones, which have a tendency to splinter into sharp, dangerous pieces. Also

playful pups. Puppies are the 'children' of the dog world, and what child does not love toys? Chew toys provide enjoyment to both dog and owner—your dog will enjoy playing with his favourite toys, whilst you will enjoy the fact that they distract him from your expensive shoes and leather sofa. Puppies love to chew; in fact, chewing is a physical need for pups as they are teething, and everything looks appetising! The full range of your possessions—from old tea towel to Oriental rug—are fair game in the eyes of a teething pup. Puppies are not all that discerning when it comes to finding something to literally 'sink their teeth into'— everything tastes great!

If the puppies were raised by a knowledgeable breeder, crate training becomes a natural continuation of the puppy's rearing. Puppies instinctively know not to relieve themselves in the places where they sleep or eat.

49

You can find a whole variety of quality, safe toys at your local pet shop. The shopkeeper can recommend which toys are the most popular and the safest for gundog breeds.

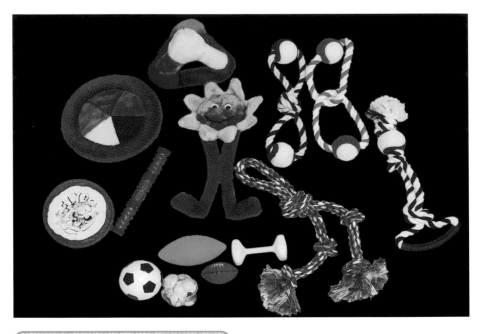

TOYS, TOYS, TOYS!

With a big variety of dog toys available, and so many that look like they would be a lot of fun for a dog, be careful in your selection. It is amazing what a set of puppy teeth can do to an innocent-looking toy, so, obviously, safety is a major consideration. Be sure to choose the most durable products that you can find. Hard nylon bones and toys are a safe bet, and many of them are offered in different scents and flavours that will be sure to capture your dog's attention. It is always fun to play a game of catch with your dog, and there are balls and flying discs that are specially made to withstand dog teeth.

be careful of rawhide, which can turn into pieces that are easy to swallow or into a mushy mess on your carpet.

LEAD

A nylon lead is probably the best option as it is the most resistant to puppy teeth should your pup take a liking to chewing on his lead. Of course, this is a habit that should be nipped in the bud, but if your pup likes to chew on his lead he has a very slim chance of being able to chew through the strong nylon. Nylon leads are also lightweight, which is good for a young Irish Setter who is just getting used to the idea of walking on a lead. For everyday walking and safety purposes, the nylon lead is a good choice. As your pup grows up and gets used to walking on the lead, you may want to purchase a flexible lead. These leads allow you to extend the length to give the dog a broader area to explore or to shorten the length to keep the dog close to you. Of course there are special leads for training purposes, but these are not necessary for routine walks.

COLLAR

Your pup should get used to wearing a collar all the time since you will want to attach his ID tags to it. You have to attach the lead to something! A lightweight nylon collar is a good choice; make sure that it fits snugly enough so that the pup cannot wriggle out of it, but is loose enough so that it will

Choose a strong but lightweight lead to walk your Irish Setter pup. Pet shops sell many different colours and styles of leads.

Although puppies will welcome almost any toy for play, owners must be careful that the chosen playthings are safe for the curious and active Irish Setter.

51

not be uncomfortably tight around the pup's neck. You should be able to fit a finger between the pup and the collar. It may take some time for your pup to get used to wearing the collar, but soon he will not even notice that it is there. Choke collars are made for training, but should only be used by an experienced handler.

FOOD AND WATER BOWLS

Your pup will need two bowls, one for food and one for water. You may want two sets of bowls, one for inside and one for outside, depending on where the dog will be fed and where he will be spending most of his time. Stainless steel bowls are popular choices. Plastic bowls are more chewable. Dogs tend not to chew on the steel variety, which can be sterilised. Some dog owners like to put their dogs' food and water bowls on a specially made elevated stand. This brings the food closer to the dog's level so he does not have to bend down as far, thus aiding his digestion and helping to guard against bloat or gastric torsion, which can affect deep-chested breeds like the Irish Setter. It is important to buy sturdy bowls since anything is in danger of being chewed by puppy teeth and you do not want your dog to be constantly chewing apart his bowl (for his safety and for your purse!).

CLEANING SUPPLIES

Until a pup is housetrained you will be doing a lot of cleaning. Accidents will occur, which is okay in the beginning because the puppy does not know any better. All you can do is be prepared to clean up any 'accidents.' Old rags, towels, newspapers and a safe disinfectant are good to have on hand.

FINANCIAL RESPONSIBILITY

Grooming tools, collars, leashes, dog beds and, of course, toys will be an expense to you when you first obtain your pup, and the cost will trickle on throughout your dog's lifetime. If your puppy damages or destroys your possessions (as most puppies surely will!) or something belonging to a neighbour, you can calculate additional expense. There is also flea and pest control, which every dog owner faces more than once. You must be able to handle the financial responsibility of owning a dog.

Choose the Appropriate Collar for Your Dog

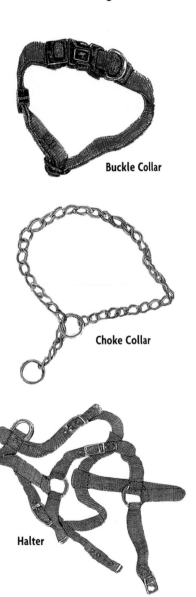

The **BUCKLE COLLAR** is the standard collar used for everyday purpose. Be sure that you adjust the buckle on growing puppies. Check it every day. It can become too tight overnight! These collars can be made of leather or nylon. Attach your dog's identification tags to this collar.

Buckle Collar

The **CHOKE COLLAR** is the usual collar recommended for training. It is constructed of highly polished steel so that it slides easily through the stainless steel loop. The idea is that the dog controls the pressure around its neck and he will stop pulling if the collar becomes uncomfortable. Never leave a choke collar on your dog when not training.

Choke Collar

The **HALTER** is for a trained dog that has to be restrained to prevent running away, chasing a cat and the like. Considered the most humane of all collars, it is frequently used on smaller dogs for which collars are not comfortable.

Halter

Stainless steel bowls are ideal for Irish Setters since they cannot chew through them and the bowls can be sterilised regularly.

For a sturdy, colourful bowl for your Irish Setter's food and water, visit your local pet shop where an array of quality pet supplies are available.

BEYOND THE BASICS

The items previously discussed are the bare necessities. You will find out what else you need as you go along—grooming supplies, flea/tick protection, baby gates to partition a room, etc. These things will vary depending on your situation but it is important that you have everything you need to feed and make your Irish Setter comfortable in his first few days at home.

PUPPY-PROOFING YOUR HOME

Aside from making sure that your Irish Setter will be comfortable in your home, you also have to make

CHEMICAL TOXINS

Scour your carport for potential puppy dangers. Remove weed killers, pesticides and antifreeze materials. Antifreeze is highly toxic and even a few drops can kill an adult dog. The sweet taste attracts the animal, who will quickly consume it from the floor or curbside.

With the right tools, cleaning up after your dog is easy. Pet shops sell a few different devices to make this task quick and efficient.

sure that your home is safe for your Irish Setter. This means taking precautions that your pup will not get into anything he should not get into and that there is nothing within his reach that may harm him should he sniff it, chew it, inspect it, etc. This probably seems obvious since, whilst you are primarily concerned with your pup's safety, at the same time you do not want your belongings to be ruined. Breakables should be placed out of reach if your dog is to have full run of the house. If he is to be limited to certain places within the house, keep any potentially dangerous items in the 'off-limits' areas. An electrical cord can pose a danger should the puppy decide to taste it—and who is going to convince a pup that it would not make a great chew toy? Cords should be fastened tightly against the wall. If your dog is going to spend time in a crate, make sure

that there is nothing near his crate that he can reach if he sticks his curious little nose or paws through the openings. Just as you would with a child, keep all household cleaners and chemicals where the pup cannot get to them.

It is also important to make sure that the outside of your home is safe. Of course your puppy should never be unsupervised, but a pup let loose in the garden will want to run and explore, and he should be granted that freedom. Do not let a fence give you a false sense of security; you would be surprised how crafty (and persistent) a dog can be in figuring out how to dig under and squeeze his way through small holes, or to jump or climb over a fence. The remedy is to make the fence high enough so that it really is impossible for your dog to get over it (about 3 metres should suffice), and well embedded into the ground. Be sure to repair or secure any gaps in the fence. Check the fence periodically to ensure that it is in good shape and make repairs as needed; a very determined pup may return to the same spot to 'work on it' until he is able to get through.

FIRST TRIP TO THE VET
You have picked out your puppy, and your home and family are ready. Now all you have to do is

An eight-week-old puppy is a helpless creature that relies upon his owner for his safety and well being. Irish Setter owners must do their part to ensure that their puppy feels comfortable and protected in its new home.

DID YOU KNOW?
You will probably start feeding your pup the same food that he has been getting from the breeder; the breeder should give you a few days' supply to start you off. Although you should not give your pup too many treats, you will want to have puppy treats on hand for coaxing, training, rewards, etc. Be careful, though, as a small pup's calorie requirements are relatively low and a few treats can add up to almost a full day's worth of calories without the required nutrition.

DID YOU KNOW?
Some experts in canine health advise that stress during a dog's early years of development can compromise and weaken his immune system and may trigger the potential for a shortened life expectancy. They emphasize the need for happy and stress-free growing-up years.

collect your Irish Setter from the breeder and the fun begins, right? Well…not so fast. Something else you need to prepare is your pup's first trip to the veterinary surgeon.

Perhaps the breeder can recommend someone in the area that specialises in Irish Setters, or maybe you know some other Irish Setter owners who can suggest a good vet. Either way, you should have an appointment arranged for your pup before you pick him up and plan on taking him for an examination before bringing him home.

The pup's first visit will consist of an overall examination to make sure that the pup does not have any problems that are not apparent to the eye. The veterinary surgeon will also set up a schedule for the pup's vaccinations; the breeder will inform you of which ones the pup has already received and the vet can continue from there.

INTRODUCTION TO THE FAMILY

Everyone in the house will be excited about the puppy coming home and will want to pet him and play with him, but it is best to make the introduction low-key so as not to overwhelm the puppy. He is apprehensive already. It is the first time he has been separated from his mother and the breeder, and the ride to your home is likely the first time he has been in a car. The last thing you want to do is smother him, as this will only frighten him further. This is not to say that human contact is not extremely necessary at this stage, because this is the time when a connection between the pup and his human family is formed. Gentle petting and soothing words should help console him, as well as just putting him down and letting him explore on his own (under your watchful eye, of course).

The pup may approach the family members or may busy himself with exploring for a while.

ELECTRICAL FENCING

The electrical fencing system which forms an invisible fence works on a battery-operated collar that shocks the dog if it gets too close to the buried (or elevated) wire. There are some people who think very highly of this system of controlling a dog's wandering. Keep in mind that the collar has batteries. For safety's sake, replace the batteries every month with the best quality batteries available.

Gradually, each person should spend some time with the pup, one at a time, crouching down to get as close to the pup's level as possible and letting him sniff their hands and petting him gently. He definitely needs human attention and he needs to be touched—this is how to form an immediate bond. Just remember that the pup is experiencing a lot of things for the first time, at the same time. There are new people, new noises, new smells, and new things to investigate: so be gentle, be affectionate, and be as comforting as you can be.

YOUR PUP'S FIRST NIGHT HOME

You have travelled home with your new charge safely in his basket or crate. He's been to the vet for a thorough check-over; he's been weighed, his papers examined; perhaps he's even been vaccinated and wormed as well. He's met the family, licked the whole family, including the excited children and the less-than-happy cat. He's explored his area, his new bed, the garden and anywhere else he's been permitted. He's eaten his first meal at home and relieved himself in the proper place. He's heard lots of new sounds, smelled new friends and seen more of the outside world than ever before.

That was just the first day! He's worn out and is ready for

bed…or so you think!

It's puppy's first night and you are ready to say 'Good night'— keep in mind that this is puppy's first night ever to be sleeping alone. His dam and littermates are no longer at paw's length and he's a bit scared, cold and lonely. Be reassuring to your new family member. This is not the time to spoil him and give in to his inevitable whining.

Puppies whine. They whine to let the others know where they are and hopefully to get company out of it. Place your pup in his new bed or crate in his room and close the door. Mercifully, he may fall asleep without a peep. If the inevitable occurs, ignore the whining: he is fine. Be strong and keep his interest in mind. Do not

allow your heart to become guilty and visit the pup. He will fall asleep.

Some breeders suggest moving the crate into your bedroom at night for the first several weeks. Sleeping in your room will not spoil the puppy. It will make him feel secure and continue the bonding process throughout the night. Beyond that, if the puppy needs to relieve himself during the night, you'll be able to whisk him out immediately. Do not ever reach in and remove him from his crate or allow him into bed with you.'

Many breeders recommend placing a piece of bedding from his former home in his new bed so that he recognises the scent of his littermates. Others still advise placing a hot water bottle in his bed for warmth. This latter may

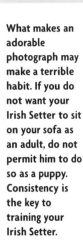

What makes an adorable photograph may make a terrible habit. If you do not want your Irish Setter to sit on your sofa as an adult, do not permit him to do so as a puppy. Consistency is the key to training your Irish Setter.

DID YOU KNOW?
The majority of problems that is commonly seen in young pups will disappear as your dog gets older. However, how you deal with problems when he is young will determine how he reacts to discipline as an adult dog. It is important to establish who is boss (hopefully it will be you!) right away when you are first bonding with your dog. This bond will set the tone for the rest of your life together.

be a good idea provided the pup doesn't attempt to suckle—he'll get good and wet and may not fall asleep so fast.

Puppy's first night can be somewhat stressful for the pup and his new family. Remember that you are setting the tone of night-time at your house. Unless you want to play with your pup every evening at 10 p.m., midnight and 2 a.m., don't initiate the habit. Your family will thank you, and so will your pup!

PREVENTING PUPPY PROBLEMS
SOCIALISATION

Now that you have done all of the preparatory work and have helped your pup get accustomed to his new home and family, it is about time for you to have some fun! Socialising your Irish Setter pup gives you the opportunity to show off your new friend, and your pup gets to reap the benefits of being an adorable furry creature that people will want to pet and, in general, think is absolutely precious!

Besides getting to know his new family, your puppy should be exposed to other people, animals and situations, but of course he must not come into close contact with dogs you don't know well until his course of injections is fully complete. This will help him become well adjusted as he grows up and less prone to being timid or fearful of the new things he will encounter. Your pup's sociali-sation began at the breeder's but now it is your responsibility to continue it. The socialisation he receives from 16 to 20 weeks is the most critical, as this is the time when he forms his impres-sions of the outside world. Be especially careful during the eight- to ten-week period, also known as the fear period. The interaction he receives during this time should be gentle and reassuring. Lack of socialisation can manifest itself in fear and aggression as the dog grows up. He needs lots of human contact, affection, handling and exposure to other animals.

Once your pup has received his necessary vaccinations, feel free to take him out and about (on his lead, of course). Walk him around the neighbourhood, take

SOCIALISATION

Thorough socialisation includes not only meeting new people but also being introduced to new experiences such as riding in the auto, having his coat brushed, hearing the television, walking in a crowd—the list is endless. The more your pup experiences, and the more positive the experiences are, the less of a shock and the less scary it will be for your pup to encounter new things.

him on your daily errands, let people pet him, let him meet other dogs and pets, etc. Puppies do not have to try to make friends; there will be no shortage of people who will want to introduce themselves. Just make sure that you carefully supervise each meeting. If the neighbour-hood children want to say hello, for example, that is great—children and pups most often make great companions. Sometimes an excited child can unintentionally handle a pup too roughly, or an overzealous pup can playfully nip a little too hard. You want to make socialisation experiences positive ones. What a pup learns during this very formative stage will impact his attitude toward future encounters. You want your dog to be comfort-able around everyone. A pup that has a bad experience with a child may grow up to be a dog that is shy around or aggressive toward children.

CONSISTENCY IN TRAINING

Dogs, being pack animals, naturally need a leader, or else they try to establish dominance in their packs. When you bring a dog into your family, the choice of who becomes the leader and who becomes the 'pack' is entirely up to you! Your pup's intuitive quest for dominance, coupled with the fact that it is nearly impossible to look at an adorable

Irish Setter pup, with his 'puppy-dog' eyes and his too-big-for his-head-still-floppy ears, and not cave in, give the pup almost an unfair advantage in getting the upper hand! A pup will definitely test the waters to see what he can and cannot do. Do not give in to those pleading

Exploring the environment is part of being a curious Irish Setter puppy. For the pup's safety, be certain that your garden is completely enclosed and properly puppy-proofed.

BOY OR GIRL?
An important consideration to be discussed is the sex of your puppy. For a family companion, a bitch may be the better choice, considering the female's inbred concern for all young creatures and her accompanying tolerance and patience. It is always advised to spay a pet bitch, which may guarantee her a longer life.

Soft chew toys are not recommended for puppies, although they can be great fun for your Irish Setter toddler. Always supervise the puppy whenever he's playing with any toy.

Mother tells him to get off the sofa when he is used to sitting up there with Father to watch the nightly news. Avoid discrepancies by having all members of the household decide on the rules before the pup even comes home...and be consistent in enforcing them! Early training shapes the dog's personality, so you cannot be unclear in what you expect.

COMMON PUPPY PROBLEMS

The best way to prevent puppy problems is to be proactive in stopping an undesirable behaviour as soon as it starts. The old saying 'You can't teach an old dog new tricks' does not necessarily hold true, but it is true that it is much easier to discourage bad behaviour in a young developing pup than to wait until the pup's bad behaviour becomes the adult dog's bad habit. There are some problems that are especially prevalent in puppies as they develop.

NIPPING

As puppies start to teethe, they feel the need to sink their teeth into anything available...unfortunately that includes your fingers,

eyes—stand your ground when it comes to disciplining the pup and make sure that all family members do the same. It will only confuse the pup when

TRAINING TIP
Training your puppy takes much patience and can be frustrating at times, but you should see results from your efforts. If you have a puppy that seems untrainable, take him to a trainer or behaviourist. The dog may have a personality problem that requires the help of a professional, or perhaps you need help in learning how to train your dog.

arms, hair, and toes. You may find this behaviour cute for the first five seconds...until you feel just how sharp those puppy teeth are. This is something you want to discourage immediately and consistently with a firm 'No!' (or whatever number of firm 'No's' it takes for him to understand that you mean business). Then replace your finger with an appropriate chew toy. Whilst this behaviour is merely annoying when the dog is young, it can become dangerous as your Irish Setter's adult teeth grow in and his jaws develop, and he continues to think it is okay to gnaw on human appendages. This is a sporting breed with a natural tendency to chew and nip. Your Irish Setter does not mean any harm with a friendly nip, but he also does not know his own strength.

CRYING/WHINING
Your pup will often cry, whine, whimper, howl or make some

NO CHOCOLATE!
Use treats to bribe your dog into a desired behaviour. Try small pieces of hard cheese or freeze-dried liver. Never offer chocolate as it has toxic qualities for dogs.

type of commotion when he is left alone. This is basically his way of calling out for attention to make sure that you know he is there and that you have not forgotten about him. He feels insecure when he is left alone,

Climbing on the furniture and becoming top dog, this Irish Setter pup may be asserting his dominance. Remember that you, the owner, must always be the leader.

when you are out of the house and he is in his crate or when you are in another part of the house and he cannot see you. The noise he is making is an expression of the anxiety he feels at being alone, so he needs to be taught that being alone is okay. You are not actually training the dog to stop making noise, you are training him to feel comfortable when he is alone and thus removing the need for him to make the noise. This is where the crate with cosy bedding and a toy comes in handy. You want to know that he is safe when you are not there to supervise, and you know that he will be safe in his crate rather than roaming freely about the house. In order for the pup to stay in his crate without making a fuss, he needs to be comfortable in his crate. On that note, it is extremely important that the crate is never used as a form of punishment, or the pup will have a negative association with the crate.

Accustom the pup to the crate in short, gradually increasing time intervals in which you put him in the crate, maybe with a treat, and stay in the room with him. If he cries or makes a fuss, do not go to him, but stay in his sight. Gradually he will realise that staying in his crate is all right without your help, and it will not be so traumatic for him when you are not around. You may want to leave the radio on softly when you leave the house; the sound of human voices may be comforting to him.

Irish Setter puppies thrive on love and attention. Use the puppy's crate to ensure the pup that he is safe and that you are always close and available. He will learn to depend on his crate for security, especially when you are away from home.

DIETARY AND FEEDING CONSIDERATIONS

Today the choices of food for your Irish Setter are many and varied. There are simply dozens of brands of food in all sorts of flavours and textures, ranging from puppy diets to those for seniors. There are even hypoallergenic and low-calorie diets available. Because your Irish Setter's food has a bearing on coat, health and temperament, it is essential that the most suitable diet is selected for an Irish Setter of his age. It is fair to say, however, that even dedicated owners can be somewhat perplexed by the enormous range of foods available. Only understanding what is best for your dog will help you reach a valued decision.

Dog foods are produced in three basic types: dried, semi-moist and tinned. Dried foods are useful for the cost-conscious for overall they tend to be less expensive than semi-moist or tinned. These contain the least fat and the most preser-vatives. In general tinned foods are made up of 60–70 percent water, whilst semi-moist ones often contain so much sugar that they are perhaps the least preferred by owners, even though their dogs seem to like them.

When selecting your dog's diet, three stages of development must be considered: the puppy stage, adult stage and the senior or veteran stage.

> **DID YOU KNOW?**
> A good test for proper diet is the colour, odour, and firmness of your dog's stool. A healthy dog usually produces three semi-hard stools per day. The stools should have no unpleasant odour. They should be the same colour from excretion to excretion.

> **DID YOU KNOW?**
> You must store your dried dog food carefully. Open packages of dog food quickly lose their vitamin value, usually within 90 days of being opened. Mould spores and vermin could also contaminate the food.

The breeder introduces the litter to cereal and meat meals around the third week. This begins the process of weaning the pups from the dam.

PUPPY STAGE

Puppies instinctively want to suck milk from their mother's teats and a normal puppy will exhibit this behaviour from just a few moments following birth. If puppies do not attempt to suckle within the first half-hour or so, they should be encouraged to do so by placing them on a nipple, having selected ones with plenty of milk. This early milk supply is important in providing colostrum to protect the puppies during the first eight to ten weeks of their lives. Although a mother's milk is much better than any milk formula, despite there being some excellent ones available, if the puppies do not feed you will have to feed them yourself. For those with less experience, advice from a veterinary surgeon is important so that you feed not only the right quantity of milk but that of correct quality, fed at suitably frequent intervals, usually every two hours during the first few days of life.

Puppies should be allowed to nurse from their mothers for about the first six weeks, although from the third or fourth week you will have begun to introduce small portions of suitable solid food. Most breeders like to introduce alternate milk and meat meals initially, building up to weaning time.

FOOD PREFERENCE

Selecting the best dried dog food is difficult. There is no majority consensus amongst veterinary scientists as to the value of nutrient analyses (protein, fat, fibre, moisture, ash, cholesterol, minerals, etc.). All agree that feeding trials are what matters, but you also have to consider the individual dog. Its weight, age, activity and what pleases its taste, all must be considered. It is probably best to take the advice of your veterinary surgeon. Every dog's dietary requirements vary, even during the lifetime of a particular dog.

If your dog is fed a good dried food, it does not require supplements of meat or vegetables. Dogs do appreciate a little variety in their diets so you may choose to stay with the same brand, but vary the flavour. Alternatively you may wish to add a little flavoured stock to give a difference to the taste.

By the time the puppies are seven or a maximum of eight weeks old, they should be fully weaned and fed solely on a proprietary puppy food. Selection of the most suitable, good-quality diet at this time is essential for a puppy's fastest growth rate is during the first year of life. Veterinary surgeons are usually able to offer advice in this regard and, although the frequency of meals will have been reduced over time, only when a young dog has reached the

Puppies at six to eight weeks of age are fed a dried food that offers them proper nourishment during the fast-growth period.

age of about 12 months should an adult diet be fed.

Puppy and junior diets should be well balanced for the needs of your dog, so that except in certain circumstances additional vitamins, minerals and proteins will not be required.

ADULT DIETS
A dog is considered an adult when it has stopped growing. Irish Setters reach physical maturity at about two years of age, although some dogs fully mature at 16 months, while other may take longer. Again you should rely upon your veterinary surgeon or dietary specialist to recommend an acceptable maintenance diet. Major dog food manufacturers specialise in this type of food, and it is just necessary for you to select the one best suited to your dog's needs. Active dogs may have different requirements than sedate dogs.

DID YOU KNOW?
Dog food must be at room temperature, neither too hot nor too cold. Fresh water, changed daily and served in a clean bowl, is mandatory, especially when feeding dried food.

Never feed your dog from the table while you are eating. Never feed your dog left-overs from your own meal. They usually contain too much fat and too much seasoning.

Dogs must chew their food. Hard pellets are excellent; soups and slurries are to be avoided.

Don't add left-overs or any extras to normal dog food. The normal food is usually balanced and adding something extra destroys the balance.

Except for age-related changes, dogs do not require dietary variations. They can be fed the same diet, day after day, without their becoming ill.

Appetites are rarely a problem in Irish Setter puppies. This young pup is stepping into his food.

SENIOR DIETS

As dogs get older, their metabolism changes. The older dog usually exercises less, moves more slowly and sleeps more.

The Irish Setter's diet needs to be consistent and balanced, regardless of the age of the dog.

IDENTIFICATION

If your dog gets lost, he is not able to ask for directions home.

Identification tags fastened to the collar give important information—the dog's name, the owner's name, the owner's address and a telephone number where the owner can be reached. This makes it easy for whom ever finds the dog to contact the owner and arrange to have the dog returned. An added advantage is that a person will be more likely to approach a lost dog who has ID tags on his collar; it tells the person that this is somebody's pet rather than a stray. This is the easiest and fastest method of identification provided that the tags stay on the collar and the collar stays on the dog.

This change in lifestyle and physiological performance requires a change in diet. Since these changes take place slowly, they might not be recognisable. What is easily recognisable is weight gain. By continuing to feed your dog an adult-maintenance diet when it is slowing down metabolically, your dog will gain weight. Obesity in an older dog compounds the health problems that already accompany old age.

As your dog gets older, few of their organs function up to par. The kidneys slow down and the intestines become less efficient. These age-related factors are best handled with a change in diet and a change in feeding schedule to

give smaller portions that are more easily digested.

There is no single best diet for every older dog. Whilst many

Water keeps the dog's body properly hydrated and promotes normal function of the body's systems. During housebreaking it is necessary to keep an eye on how much water your Irish Setter is drinking, but once he is reliably trained he should have access to clean fresh water at all times. Make sure that the dog's water bowl is clean, and change the water often, making sure that water is always available for your dog, especially if you feed dried food.

Fresh water must be offered to your dog at all times. Owners want to monitor their puppy's water intake so that they can better predict the toilet times.

dogs do well on light or senior diets, other dogs do better on puppy diets or other special premium diets such as lamb and rice. Be sensitive to your senior Irish Setter's diet and this will help control other problems that may arise with your old friend.

WATER
Just as your dog needs proper nutrition from his food, water is an essential 'nutrient' as well.

EXERCISE
All dogs require some form of exercise, regardless of breed. The Irish Setter is a field dog with an

GRAIN-BASED DIETS
Many adult diets are based on grain. There is nothing wrong with this as long as it does not contain soy meal. Diets based on soy often cause flatulence (passing gas).

Grain-based diets are almost always the least expensive and a good grain diet is just as good as the most expensive diet containing animal protein.

There are many cases, however, when your dog might require a special diet. These special requirements should only be recommended by your veterinary surgeon.

Many breeders advise moistening the dried food with warm water to add to the puppy's enjoyment.

69

What are you feeding your dog?

Read the label on your dog food. Many dog foods only advise what 50—55% of the contents are, leaving the other 45% in doubt.

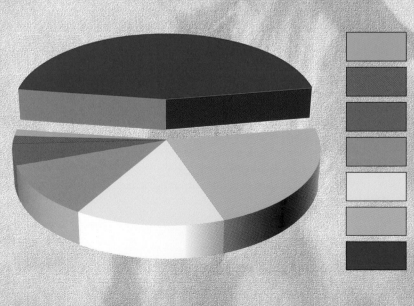

1.3% Calcium

1.6% Fatty Acids

4.6% Crude Fibre

11% Moisture

14% Crude Fat

22% Crude Protein

45.5% ? ? ?

abundance of energy and enthusiasm. A sedentary lifestyle is as harmful to a dog as it is to a person. The Irish Setter happens to be a very active breed that enjoys exercise. Long daily walks, play sessions in the garden, or letting the dog run free in the garden under your supervision are sufficient forms of exercise for the Irish Setter. Bear in mind that an Irish Setter needs about two hours of exercise per day. For those who are more ambitious, you will find that your Irish Setter also enjoys long walks, an occasional hike or even a swim! Bear in mind that an overweight dog should never be suddenly over-exercised; instead he should be allowed to increase exercise slowly. Not only is exercise essential to keep the dog's body fit, it is essential to his mental well being. A bored dog will find something to do, which often manifests itself in some type of destructive behaviour.

GROOMING

Regular grooming sessions are also a good way to spend time with your dog. The Irish Setter coat is one of his most distinguished features. Although proper diet and exercise are necessary to maintain that satin sheen, regular grooming and trimming are also needed to keep it looking neat and trim. Brushing will remove dead hair and stimulate the natural oils to keep the shine in the Irish

Long daily walks with the Irish Setter ensures good health for dog and owner alike. This healthy trio enjoy that special bonding time every morning and evening.

Setter coat. Twice a week brushing is a healthy protocol to follow.

You will need some grooming equipment to maintain your Irish Setter's coat. You will need are two combs with handles—one wide-tooth for going over the coat and one fine-tooth for the

DID YOU KNOW?
You should be careful where you exercise your dog. Many countryside areas have been sprayed with chemicals that are highly toxic to both dogs and humans. Never allow your dog to eat grass or drink from puddles on either public or private grounds, as the run-off water may contain chemicals from sprays and herbicides.

71

Your local pet shop will have a variety of grooming tools, brushes and combs that will assist you in keeping your Irish Setter's coat in good condition.

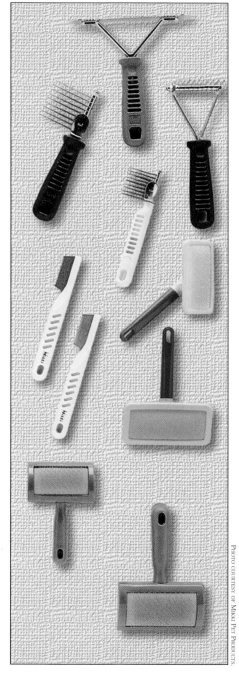

PHOTO COURTESY OF MIKKI PET PRODUCTS.

undercoat. A natural bristle brush is used for polishing the body coat and the feathering. Thinning shears should be used to trim excess hair from the ears and neck and behind the ears, and on the feet and hocks. A straight scissors is used to trim out feathering on the feet and tail.

Before any grooming session, always first check the coat for matts and tangles. Remove them with gentle brushing or with a detangling spray available from your local grooming parlour. Always brush or comb the coat in the direction in which it lies. Use the comb first to remove any mud or debris, and follow with a thorough body brushing. Use a spray conditioner on the brush

GROOMING EQUIPMENT

How much grooming equipment you purchase will depend on how much grooming you are going to do. Here are some basics:

- Natural bristle brush
- Wide- and fine-tooth comb
- Scissors
- Blaster
- Rubber mat
- Dog shampoo
- Spray hose attachment
- Ear cleaner
- Cotton wipes
- Towels
- Nail clippers
- Thinning shears

which will enhance the coat condition.

To trim the Irish Setter's ears, hold the ear up and thin the hair behind and underneath the ear. Thin in an upward direction, and comb out after every cut as you thin to check on your progress. Trim the inside of the ear as well, being especially careful not to cut the skin. To trim the feathering on the topside of the ear, thin only from underneath to prevent unsightly scissor lines on top. After thinning, use the straight scissors to neaten up the line around the ear. While atop the head, check also for dead coat on the dog's skull. Never scissor cut atop the head; rather, pluck dead or stray hairs with your fingers. To trim the neck, again use your thinning scissors in an upward cut, always combing with each cut. To neaten dog's feet, use your straight scissors to first trim the excess hair from the bottom of the pads, then cut around the toes to define the outline of the foot. Thin any excess feathering between the toes. Now move to the feathering on the hocks. Comb and brush it thoroughly in an upward direction. Use the thinning scissors in a downward direction, and continue to comb as you thin.

The lovely Irish Setter tail deserves your special attention. Hold it up and brush carefully with a bristle brush. Fold the tail feathering around the tail and

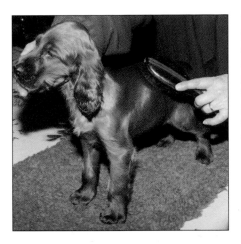

Train the puppy to stand to be combed. Provide a non-slip surface on a table so that the puppy is not afraid or anxious about grooming.

Comb through the feathering under the dog's belly to keep it free from matts and tangles.

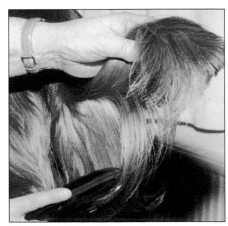

The tail can become tangled if not combed through regularly.

Keeping the Irish Setter's coat glistening and clean requires regular brushing and occasional bathing.

A soft-bristle brush is effective on the neck and chest fringe.

trim the excess hair from the tip of the tail to an even taper. Trim the feathering with a straight scissors to a gradual taper from the rear out to the tip.

To become more proficient in grooming your Irish Setter, schedule an appointment with a groomer for a lesson in keeping your dog's coat in top condition.

BATHING

Dogs do not need to be bathed as often as humans, but regular bathing is essential for healthy skin and a healthy, shiny coat. Again, like most anything, if you accustom your pup to being bathed as a puppy, it will be second nature by the time he grows up. You want your dog to be at ease in the bath or else it could end up a wet, soapy, messy ordeal for both of you!

Brush your Irish Setter thoroughly before wetting his

DID YOU KNOW?

The use of human soap products like shampoo, bubble bath and hand soap can be damaging to a dog's coat and skin. Human products are too strong and remove the protective oils coating the dog's hair and skin (making him water-resistant). Use only shampoo made especially for dogs and you may like to use a medicated shampoo, which will always help to keep external parasites at bay.

coat. This will get rid of most matts and tangles, which are harder to remove when the coat is wet. Make sure that your dog has a good non-slip surface to stand on. Begin by wetting the dog's coat. A shower or hose attachment is necessary for thoroughly wetting and rinsing the coat. Check the water temperature to make sure that it is neither too hot nor too cold.

Next, apply shampoo to the dog's coat and work it into a good lather. You should purchase a shampoo that is made for dogs. Do not use a product made for human hair. Wash the head last; you do not want shampoo to drip into the dog's eyes whilst you are washing

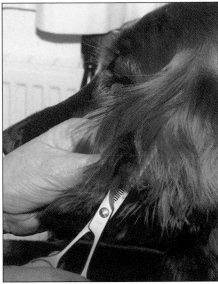

Use a thinning shears to trim the Irish Setter's ears, thinning in an upward direction. On the top side of the ear, only thin from underneath to prevent unsightly scissor lines.

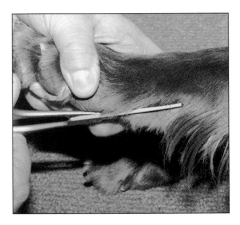

The feet can be neatened by using a straight scissors, trimming in a downward direction.

Remove excess hair from between the toes with your scissors.

GROOMING TIP

Once you are sure that the dog is thoroughly rinsed, squeeze the excess water out of the coat with your hand and dry him with a heavy towel. You may choose to use a blaster on his coat or just let it dry naturally. In cold weather, never allow your dog outside with a wet coat.

There are 'dry bath' products on the market, which are sprays and powders intended for spot cleaning, that can be used between regular baths, if necessary. They are not substitutes for regular baths, but they are easy to use for touch-ups as they do not require rinsing.

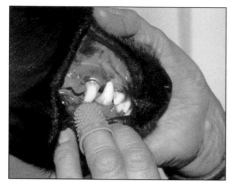

Teeth are forever! Don't forget to attend to your Irish Setter's teeth in your grooming routine. This chap's choppers are pearly white, from regular brushing and dental visits.

the rest of his body. Work the shampoo all the way down to the skin. You can use this opportunity to check the skin for any bumps, bites or other abnormalities. Do not neglect any area of the body—get all of the hard-to-reach places.

Once the dog has been thoroughly shampooed, he requires an equally thorough rinsing. Shampoo left in the coat can be irritating to the skin. Protect his eyes from the shampoo by shielding them with your hand and directing the flow of water in the opposite direction. You should also avoid getting water in the ear canal. Be prepared for your dog to shake out his coat—you might want to stand back, but make sure you have a hold on the dog to keep him from running through the house.

EAR CLEANING

The ears should be kept clean and any excess hair inside the ear should be plucked carefully out. Ears can be cleaned with special

cottoncleaning wipes made for dogs. Be on the lookout for any signs of infection or ear mite infestation. If your Irish Setter has been shaking his head or scratching at his ears frequently, this usually indicates a problem. If his ears have an unusual odour, this is a sure sign of mite infestation or infection, and a signal to have his ears checked by the veterinary surgeon.

NAIL CLIPPING

Your Irish Setter should be accustomed to having his nails trimmed at an early age, since it will be part of your maintenance routine throughout his life. Not only does it look nicer, but long nails can scratch someone unintentionally. Also, a long nail has a better chance of ripping and bleeding, or causing the feet to spread. A good rule of thumb is that if you can hear your dog's nails clicking on the floor when he walks, his nails are too long.

Before you start cutting, make sure you can identify the 'quick' in each nail. The quick is a blood vessel that runs through the centre of each nail and grows rather close to the end. It will bleed if accidentally cut, which will be quite painful for the dog as it contains nerve endings. Keep some type of clotting agent on hand, such as a styptic pencil or styptic powder (the type used for shaving). This will stop the bleeding quickly when applied to the end of the cut nail. Do not panic if this happens, just stop the bleeding and talk soothingly to your dog. Once he has calmed down, move on to the next nail. It is better to clip a little at a time, particularly with black-nailed dogs.

Hold your pup steady as you begin trimming his nails; you do not want him to make any sudden movements or run away. Talk to him soothingly and stroke him as you clip. Holding his foot in your hand, simply take off the end of each nail in one quick clip. You can purchase nail clippers that are specially made for dogs; you can probably find them wherever you buy pet or grooming supplies.

TRAVELLING WITH YOUR DOG
CAR TRAVEL
You should accustom your Irish Setter to riding in a car at an early age. You may or may not take him

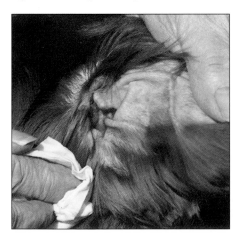

When introduced to the nail clipping routine as a pup, the adult Irish Setter will be patient and co-operative.

in the car often, but at the very least he will need to go to the vet and you do not want these trips to be traumatic for the dog or a big hassle for you. The safest way for a dog to ride in the car is in his crate. If he uses a crate in the

DID YOU KNOW?
A dog that spends a lot of time outside on a hard surface, such as cement or pavement, will have his nails naturally worn down and may not need to have them trimmed as often, except maybe in the colder months when he is not outside as much. Regardless, it is best to get your dog accustomed to this procedure at an early age so that he is used to it. Some dogs are especially sensitive about having their feet touched, but if a dog has experienced it since he was young, he should not be bothered by it.

Use a cotton wipe to clean any excess debris from your Irish Setter's ears. Regular attention to ear cleaning will prevent infection, bad odours and parasites.

77

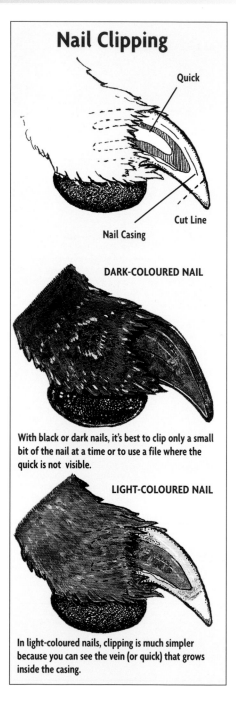

Nail Clipping

Quick

Cut Line

Nail Casing

DARK-COLOURED NAIL

With black or dark nails, it's best to clip only a small bit of the nail at a time or to use a file where the quick is not visible.

LIGHT-COLOURED NAIL

In light-coloured nails, clipping is much simpler because you can see the vein (or quick) that grows inside the casing.

house, you can use the same crate for travel, if your vehicle can accommodate it. Put the pup in the crate and see how he reacts. If the puppy seems uneasy, you can have a passenger hold him on his lap whilst you drive but you will need to find another solution by the time your dog is fully grown. Another option is a specially made safety harness for dogs, which straps the dog in much like a seat belt. Do not let the dog roam loose in the vehicle—this is very dangerous! If you should stop short, your dog can be thrown and injured. If the dog starts climbing on you and pestering you whilst you are driving, you will not be able to concentrate on the road. It is an unsafe situation for everyone— human and canine.

For long trips, be prepared to stop to let the dog relieve himself. Bring along whatever you need to clean up after him. You should take along some paper kitchen towels and perhaps some old

TRAVEL TIP
Never leave your dog alone in the car. In hot weather your dog can die from the high temperature inside a closed vehicle; even a car parked in the shade can heat up very quickly. Leaving the window open is dangerous as well since the dog can hurt himself trying to get out.

towelling for use should he have an accident in the car or suffer from travel sickness.

AIR TRAVEL

Whilst it is possible to take a dog on a flight within Britain, this is fairly unusual and advance permission is always required. The dog will be required to travel in a fibreglass crate and you should always check in advance with the airline regarding specific

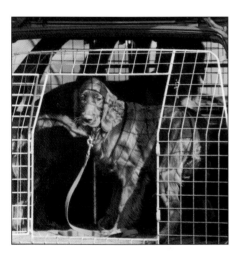

TRAVEL TIP
When travelling, never let your dog off-lead in a strange area. Your dog could run away out of fear or decide to chase a passing chipmunk or cat or simply want to stretch his legs without restriction—you might never see your canine friend again.

TRAVEL TIP
If you are going on a long motor trip with your dog, be sure the hotels are dog friendly. Many hotels do not accept dogs. Also take along some ice that can be thawed and offered to your dog if he becomes overheated. Most dogs like to lick ice.

requirements. To help the dog be at ease, put one of his favourite toys in the crate with him. Do not feed the dog for at least six hours before the trip to minimise his need to relieve himself. However, certain regulations specify that water must always be made available to the dog in the crate.

Make sure your dog is properly identified and that your contact information appears on his ID tags and on his crate. Animals travel in a different area of the plane than human passengers so every rule must be strictly adhered to so as to prevent the risk of getting separated from your dog.

When travelling with your Irish Setter, select a method that is safe and convenient. Using a crate is the method of choice, provided your vehicle can accommodate the size crate you need for a full-grown Irish Setter.

BOARDING

So you want to take a family holiday—and you want to include all members of the family. You would probably make arrangements for accommodations ahead of time anyway, but this is especially important when travelling with a dog. You do not want to make an overnight stop at the only place around for miles and find out that they do not allow dogs. Also, you do not want to reserve a place for your family without confirming that you are travelling with a dog because if it is against their policy you may not have a place to stay.

Alternatively, if you are travelling and choose not to bring your Irish Setter, you will have to make arrangements for him whilst you are away. Some options are to take him to a neighbour's house to stay whilst you are gone, to have a trusted neighbour stop by often or stay at your house, or bring your dog to a reputable boarding kennel. If you choose to board him at a kennel, you should visit in advance to see the facility, how

TRAVEL TIP

For international travel you will have to make arrangements well in advance (perhaps months), as countries' regulations pertaining to bringing in animals differ. There may be special health certificates and/or vaccinations that your dog will need before taking the trip, sometimes this has to be done within a certain time frame. In rabies-free countries, you will need to bring proof of the dog's rabies vaccination and there may be a quarantine period upon arrival.

DID YOU KNOW?

As puppies become more and more expensive, especially those puppies of high quality for showing and/or breeding, they have a greater chance of being stolen. The usual collar dog tag is, of course, easily removed. But there are two techniques that have become widely utilised for identification.

The puppy microchip implantation involves the injection of a small microchip, about the size of a corn kernel, under the skin of the dog. If your dog shows up at a clinic or shelter, or is offered for resale under less than savory circumstances, it can be positively identified by the microchip. The microchip is scanned and a registry quickly identifies you as the owner. This is not only protection against theft, but should the dog run away or go chasing a squirrel and get lost, you have a fair chance of getting it back.

Tattooing is done on various parts of the dog, from its belly to its cheeks. The number tattooed can be your telephone number or any other number which you can easily memorise. When professional dog thieves see a tattooed dog, they usually lose interest in it. Both microchipping and tattooing can be done at your local veterinary clinic. For the safety of our dogs, no laboratory facility or dog broker will accept a tattooed dog as stock.

clean they are and where the dogs are kept. Talk to some of the employees and see how they treat the dogs—do they spend time with the dogs, play with them, exercise them, etc.? Also find out the kennel's policy on vaccinations and what they require. This is for all of the dogs' safety, since when dogs are kept together, there is a greater risk of diseases being passed from dog to dog.

IDENTIFICATION

Your Irish Setter is your valued companion and friend. That is why you always keep a close eye on him and you have made sure that he cannot escape from the garden or wriggle out of his collar and run away from you. However,

accidents can happen and there may come a time when your dog unexpectedly gets separated from you. If this unfortunate event should occur, the first thing on your mind will be finding him. Proper identification, including an ID tag, a tattoo, and possibly a microchip, will increase the chances of his being returned to you safely and quickly.

DID YOU KNOW?

You have a valuable dog. If the dog is lost or stolen, you would undoubtedly become extremely upset. If you encounter a lost dog, notify the police or the local animal shelter.

Living with an untrained dog is a lot like owning a piano that you do not know how to play—it is a nice object to look at but it does not do much more than that to bring you pleasure. Now try taking piano lessons and suddenly the piano comes alive and brings forth magical sounds and rhythms that set your heart singing and your body swaying.

The same is true with your Irish Setter. Any dog is a big responsibility and if not trained sensibly may develop unacceptable behaviour that annoys you or could even cause family friction.

To train your Irish Setter, you may like to enrol in an obedience class. Teach him good manners as you learn how and why he behaves the way he does. Find out how to communicate with your dog and how to recognise and understand his communications with you. Suddenly the dog takes on a new role in your life—he is smart, interesting, well behaved and fun to be with. He demonstrates his bond of devotion to you daily. In other words, your Irish Setter does wonders for your ego because he constantly reminds you that you are not only his leader, you are his hero!

Those involved with teaching dog obedience and counselling owners about their dogs' behaviour have discovered some interesting facts about dog ownership. For example, training dogs when they are puppies results in the highest rate of success in developing well-mannered and well-adjusted adult dogs. Training an older dog, from six months to six years of age, can produce almost equal results provided that the owner accepts the dog's slower rate of learning capability and is willing to work patiently to help the dog succeed at developing to his fullest potential. Unfortunately, many owners of untrained adult dogs

DID YOU KNOW?

If you start with a normal, healthy dog and give him time, patience and some carefully executed lessons, you will reap the rewards of that training for the life of the dog. And what a life it will be! The two of you will find immeasurable pleasure in the companionship you have built together with love, respect and understanding.

DID YOU KNOW?

To a dog's way of thinking, your hands are like his mouth in terms of a defence mechanism. If you squeeze him too tightly, he might just bite you because that would be his normal response. This is not aggressive biting and, although all biting should be discouraged, you need the discipline in learning how to handle your dog.

lack the patience factor, so they do not persist until their dogs are successful at learning particular behaviours.

Training a puppy aged 10 to 16 weeks (20 weeks at the most) is like working with a dry sponge in a pool of water. The pup soaks up whatever you show him and constantly looks for more things to do and learn. At this early age, his body is not yet producing hormones, and therein lies the reason for such a high rate of success. Without hormones, he is focused on his owners and not particularly interested in investigating other places, dogs, people, etc. You are his leader: his provider of food, water, shelter and security. He latches onto you and wants to stay close. He will usually follow you from room to room, will not let you out of his sight when you are outdoors with him, and will respond in like

manner to the people and animals you encounter. If you greet a friend warmly, he will be happy to greet the person as well. If, however, you are hesitant, even anxious, about the approach of a stranger, he will respond accordingly.

Once the puppy begins to produce hormones, his natural curiosity emerges and he begins to investigate the world around him. It is at this time when you may notice that the untrained dog begins to wander away from you and even ignore your commands to stay close.

There are usually classes within a reasonable distance of the owner's home, but you can also do a lot to train your dog yourself. Sometimes there are classes available but the tuition is too costly. Whatever the circumstances, the solution to the problem of lack of lesson availability lies within the pages of this book.

TRAINING TIP

Training a dog is a life experience. Many parents admit that much of what they know about raising children they learned from caring for their dogs. Dogs respond to love, fairness and guidance, just as children do. Become a good dog owner and you may become an even better parent.

83

This chapter is devoted to helping you train your Irish Setter at home. If the recommended procedures are followed faithfully, you may expect positive results that will prove rewarding to both you and your dog.

Whether your new charge is a puppy or a mature adult, the methods of teaching and the techniques we use in training basic behaviours are the same. After all, no dog, whether puppy or adult, likes harsh or inhumane methods. All creatures, however, respond favourably to gentle motivational methods and sincere praise and encouragement. Now let us get started.

All dogs need structure as well as motivation. Engrain a routine into your puppy's world and give him plenty of love and you will have a delightful Irish Setter adult in no time at all.

HOUSEBREAKING

You can train a puppy to relieve itself wherever you choose, but this must be somewhere suitable. You should bear in mind from the outset that when your puppy is old enough to go out in public

MEALTIME
Mealtime should be a peaceful time for your puppy. Do not put his food and water bowls in a high-traffic area in the house. For example, give him his own little corner of the kitchen where he can eat undisturbed and where he will not be under foot. Do not allow small children or other family members to disrupt the pup when he is eating.

places, any canine deposits must be removed at once. You will always have to carry with you a small plastic bag or 'poop-scoop.'

Outdoor training includes such surfaces as grass, dirt and cement. Indoor training usually means training your dog to newspaper.

When deciding on the surface and location that you will want your Irish Setter to use, be sure it is going to be permanent. Training

THINK BEFORE YOU BARK
Dogs are sensitive to their master's moods and emotions. Use your voice wisely when communicating with your dog. Never raise your voice at your dog unless you are angry and trying to correct him. 'Barking' at your dog can become as meaningless as 'dogspeak' is to you. Think before you bark!

your dog to grass and then changing your mind two months later is extremely difficult for both dog and owner.

Next, choose the command you will use each and every time you want your puppy to void. 'Hurry up' and 'Toilet' are examples of commands commonly used by dog owners.

Get in the habit of giving the puppy your chosen relief command before you take him out. That way, when he becomes an adult, you will be able to determine if he wants to go out

when you ask him. A confirmation will be signs of interest, wagging his tail, watching you intently, going to the door, etc.

PUPPY'S NEEDS

Puppy needs to relieve himself after play periods, after each meal, after he has been sleeping and any time he indicates that he is looking for a place to urinate or defecate.

The urinary and intestinal tract muscles of very young puppies are not fully developed. Therefore, like human babies, puppies need to relieve themselves frequently.

Take your puppy out often— every hour for an eight-week-old, for example, and always immediately after sleeping and eating. The older the puppy, the less often he will need to relieve himself. Finally, as a mature healthy adult, he will require only three to five relief trips per day.

Clean up after your Irish Setter, especially when you are in a public place. Dog owners must respect the rights of others in the community.

HOUSING

Since the types of housing and control you provide for your puppy have a direct relationship on the success of housetraining, we consider the various aspects of both before we begin training.

Bringing a new puppy home and turning him loose in your house can be compared to turning a child loose in a sports arena and telling the child that the place is all his! The sheer enormity of the place would be too much for him to handle.

Instead, offer the puppy clearly defined areas where he can play, sleep, eat and live. A room of the house where the family gathers is the most obvious choice. Puppies are social animals and need to feel a part of the pack

Puppies need time outdoors— to expend energy and to relieve themselves. Remember that your Irish Setter puppy cannot control his bladder as long as an adult. Take him out frequently.

TRAINING TIP
Your dog is actually training you at the same time you are training him. Dogs do things to get attention. They usually repeat whatever succeeds in getting your attention.

DID YOU KNOW?
Never line your pup's sleeping area with newspaper. Puppy litters are usually raised on newspaper and, once in your home, the puppy will immediately associate newspaper with voiding. Never put newspaper on any floor while housetraining, as this will only confuse the puppy. If you are paper-training him, use paper in his designated relief area ONLY. Finally, restrict water intake after evening meals. Offer a few licks at a time—never let a young puppy gulp water after meals.

right from the start. Hearing your voice, watching you whilst you are doing things and smelling you nearby are all positive reinforcers that he is now a member of your pack. Usually a family room, the kitchen or a nearby adjoining breakfast area is ideal for providing safety and security for both puppy and owner.

Within that room there should be a smaller area which the puppy can call his own. An alcove, a wire or fibreglass dog crate or a fenced (not boarded!) corner from which he can view the activities of his new family will be fine. The

Canine Development Schedule

It is important to understand how and at what age a puppy develops into adulthood. If you are a puppy owner, consult the following Canine Development Schedule to determine the stage of development your puppy is currently experiencing. This knowledge will help you as you work with the puppy in the weeks and months ahead.

Period	Age	Characteristics
FIRST TO THIRD	BIRTH TO SEVEN WEEKS	Puppy needs food, sleep and warmth, and responds to simple and gentle touching. Needs mother for security and disciplining. Needs littermates for learning and interacting with other dogs. Pup learns to function within a pack and learns pack order of dominance. Begin socialising with adults and children for short periods. Begins to become aware of its environment.
FOURTH	EIGHT TO TWELVE WEEKS	Brain is fully developed. Needs socialising with outside world. Remove from mother and littermates. Needs to change from canine pack to human pack. Human dominance necessary. Fear period occurs between 8 and 16 weeks. Avoid fright and pain.
FIFTH	THIRTEEN TO SIXTEEN WEEKS	Training and formal obedience should begin. Less association with other dogs, more with people, places, situations. Period will pass easily if you remember this is pup's change-to-adolescence time. Be firm and fair. Flight instinct prominent. Permissiveness and over-disciplining can do permanent damage. Praise for good behaviour.
JUVENILE	FOUR TO EIGHT MONTHS	Another fear period about 7 to 8 months of age. It passes quickly, but be cautious of fright and pain. Sexual maturity reached. Dominant traits established. Dog should understand sit, down, come and stay by now.

NOTE: THESE ARE APPROXIMATE TIME FRAMES. ALLOW FOR INDIVIDUAL DIFFERENCES IN PUPPIES.

An open crate is fine for inside the home. For puppies, however, never leave water in the crate as this invites accidents when the pup is crated.

Your Irish Setter puppy will become accustomed to relieving himself on grass (or whatever surface you provide). Once house-trained, he will always seek out that surface to relieve himself.

size of the area or crate is the key factor here. The area must be large enough for the puppy to lie down and stretch out as well as stand up without rubbing his head on the top, yet small enough so that he cannot relieve himself at one end and sleep at the other without coming into contact with his droppings until fully trained to relieve himself outside.

Dogs are, by nature, clean animals and will not remain close to their relief areas unless forced to do so. In those cases, they then become dirty dogs and usually remain that way for life.

The designated area should be

TRAINING TIP
Stand up straight and authoritatively when giving your dog commands. Do not issue commands when lying on the floor or lying on your back on the sofa. If you are on your hands and knees when you give a command, your dog will think you are positioning yourself to play.

HOUSEBREAKING TIP

Do not carry your dog to his toilet area. Lead him there on a leash or, better yet, encourage him to follow you to the spot. If you start carrying him to his spot, you might end up doing this routine forever and your dog will have the satisfaction of having trained YOU.

lined with clean bedding along with a toy. Water must always be available, in a non-spill container.

CONTROL

By control, we mean helping the puppy to create a lifestyle pattern that will be compatible to that of his human pack (YOU!). Just as we guide little children to learn our way of life, we must show the puppy when it is time to play, eat, sleep, exercise and even entertain himself.

Your puppy should always sleep in his crate. He should also learn that, during times of household confusion and

PRACTICE MAKES PERFECT!

• Have training lessons with your dog every day in several short segments— three to five times a day for a few minutes at a time is ideal.
• Do not have long practice sessions. The dog will become easily bored.
• Never practise when you are tired, ill, worried or in an otherwise negative mood. This will transmit to the dog and may have an adverse effect on its performance.

Think fun, short and above all POSITIVE! End each session on a high note, rather than a failed exercise, and make sure to give a lot of praise. Enjoy the training and help your dog enjoy it, too.

excessive human activity such as at breakfast when family members are preparing for the day, he can play by himself in relative safety and comfort in his designated area. Each time you leave the puppy alone, he should understand exactly where he is to stay. You can gradually increase the time he is left alone to get him used to it. Puppies are chewers. They cannot tell the difference between lamp cords, television wires, shoes, table legs, etc. Chewing into a television wire, for example, can be fatal to the puppy whilst a shorted wire can

THE SUCCESS METHOD

Success that comes by luck is usually short lived. Success that comes by well-thought-out proven methods is often more easily achieved and permanent. This is the Success Method. It is designed to give you, the puppy owner, a simple yet proven way to help your puppy develop clean living habits and a feeling of security in his new environment.

THE SUCCESS METHOD
6 Steps to Successful Crate Training

1 Tell the puppy 'Crate time!' and place him in the crate with a small treat (a piece of cheese or half of a biscuit). Let him stay in the crate for five minutes while you are in the same room. Then release him and praise lavishly. Never release him when he is fussing. Wait until he is quiet before you let him out.

2 Repeat Step 1 several times a day.

3 The next day, place the puppy in the crate as before. Let him stay there for ten minutes. Do this several times.

4 Continue building time in five-minute increments until the puppy

stays in his crate for 30 minutes with you in the room. Always take him to his relief area after prolonged periods in his crate.

5 Now go back to Step 1 and let the puppy stay in his crate for five minutes, this time while you are out of the room.

6 Once again, build crate time in five-minute increments with you out of the room. When the puppy will stay willingly in his crate (he may even fall asleep!) for 30 minutes with you out of the room, he will be ready to stay in it for several hours at a time.

HOW MANY TIMES A DAY?

AGE	RELIEF TRIPS
To 14 weeks	10
14–22 weeks	8
22–32 weeks	6
Adulthood (dog stops growing)	4

These are estimates, of course, but they are a guide to the MINIMUM opportunities a dog should have each day to relieve itself.

start a fire in the house.

If the puppy chews on the arm of the chair when he is alone, you will probably discipline him angrily when you get home. Thus, he makes the association that your coming home means he is going to be punished. (He will not remember chewing up the chair and is incapable of making the association of the discipline with his naughty deed.)

Other times of excitement, such as family parties, etc., can be fun for the puppy providing he can view the activities from the security of his designated area. He is not underfoot and he is not being fed all sorts of titbits that will probably cause him stomach distress, yet he still feels a part of the fun.

SCHEDULE

A puppy should be taken to his relief area each time he is

released from his designated area, after meals, after a play session, when he first awakens in the morning (at age eight weeks, this

Housetraining male dogs tends to be more difficult than female dogs. Males mark their territory with urine to tell other dogs that they have been there. This instinctive behaviour makes males more distracted about their toilet habits.

can mean 5 a.m.!). The puppy will indicate that he's ready 'to go' by circling or sniffing busily—do not misinterpret these signs. For a puppy less than ten weeks

DID YOU KNOW?

By providing sleeping and resting quarters that fit the dog, and offering frequent opportunities to relieve himself outside his quarters, the puppy quickly learns that the outdoors (or the newspaper if you are training him to paper) is the place to go when he needs to urinate or defecate. It also reinforces his innate desire to keep his sleeping quarters clean. This, in turn, helps develop the muscle control that will eventually produce a dog with clean living habits.

of age, a routine of taking him out every hour is necessary. As the puppy grows, he will be able to wait for longer periods of time.

Keep trips to his relief area short. Stay no more than five or six minutes and then return to the house. If he goes during that time, praise him lavishly and take him indoors immediately. If he does not, but he has an accident when you go back indoors, pick him up immediately, say 'No! No!' and return to his relief area. Wait a few minutes, then return to the house again. Never hit a puppy or rub his face in urine or excrement when he has an accident!

Once indoors, put the puppy in his crate until you have had time to clean up his accident. Then release him to the family

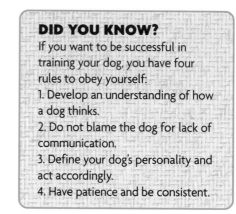

DID YOU KNOW?

If you want to be successful in training your dog, you have four rules to obey yourself:
1. Develop an understanding of how a dog thinks.
2. Do not blame the dog for lack of communication.
3. Define your dog's personality and act accordingly.
4. Have patience and be consistent.

area and watch him more closely than before. Chances are, his accident was a result of your not picking up his signal or waiting too long before offering him the opportunity to relieve himself. Never hold a grudge against the puppy for accidents.

Let the puppy learn that going outdoors means it is time to relieve himself, not play. Once trained, he will be able to play indoors and out and still differentiate between the times for play versus the times for relief.

Help him develop regular hours for naps, being alone, playing by himself and just resting, all in his crate. Encourage him to entertain himself whilst you are busy with your activities. Let him learn that having you near is comforting, but it is not your main purpose in life to provide him with undivided attention.

Each time you put a puppy in

DID YOU KNOW?

The puppy should also have regular play and exercise sessions when he is with you or a family member. Exercise for a very young puppy can consist of a short walk around the house or garden. Playing can include fetching games with a large ball or a special raggy. (All puppies teethe and need soft things upon which to chew.) Remember to restrict play periods to indoors within his living area (the family room for example) until he is completely housetrained.

his own area, use the same command, whatever suits best. Soon, he will run to his crate or special area when he hears you say those words.

Crate training provides safety for you, the puppy and the home. It also provides the puppy with a feeling of security, and that helps the puppy achieve self-confidence and clean habits.

Remember that one of the primary ingredients in housetraining your puppy is control. Regardless of your lifestyle, there will always be occasions when you will need to have a place where your dog can stay and be happy and safe. Crate training is the answer for now and in the future.

In conclusion, a few key elements are really all you need for a successful housetraining method—consistency, frequency, praise, control and supervision. By following these procedures with a normal healthy puppy,

you and the puppy will soon be past the stage of 'accidents' and ready to move on to a full and rewarding life together.

ROLES OF DISCIPLINE, REWARD AND PUNISHMENT
Discipline, training one to act in accordance with rules, brings

DID YOU KNOW?
Dogs do not understand our language. They can be trained to react to a certain sound, at a certain volume. If you say 'No, Oliver' in a very soft pleasant voice it will not have the same meaning as 'No, Oliver!!' when you shout it as loud as you can. You should never use the dog's name during a reprimand, just the command NO!! Since dogs don't understand words, comics use dogs trained with opposite meanings. Thus, when the comic commands his dog to SIT the dog will stand up; and vice versa.

You can be certain that after vigorous exercise, your Irish Setter puppy will need to relieve himself. Don't allow your puppy to confuse toilet breaks with playtime.

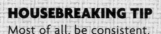

HOUSEBREAKING TIP

Most of all, be consistent. Always take your dog to the same location, always use the same command, and always have him on lead when he is in his relief area, unless a fenced-in garden is available.

By following the Success Method, your puppy will be completely housetrained by the time his muscle and brain development reach maturity. Keep in mind that small breeds usually mature faster than large breeds, but all puppies should be trained by six months of age.

order to life. It is as simple as that. Without discipline, particularly in a group society, chaos reigns supreme and the group will eventually perish. Humans and canines are social animals and need some form of discipline in order to function effectively. They must procure food, protect their home base and their young and reproduce to keep the species going.

If there were no discipline in the lives of social animals, they would eventually die from starvation and/or predation by other stronger animals.

In the case of domestic canines, dogs need discipline in their lives in order to understand how their pack (you and other family members)

functions and how they must act in order to survive.

A large humane society in a highly populated area recently surveyed dog owners regarding their satisfaction with their relationships with their dogs. People who had trained their dogs were 75% more satisfied with their pets than those who had never trained their dogs.

Dr Edward Thorndike, a psychologist, established *Thorndike's Theory of Learning*, which states that a behaviour that results in a pleasant event tends to be repeated. A behaviour that results in an unpleasant event tends not to be repeated. It is this theory on which training methods are based today. For example, if you manipulate a dog to perform a specific behaviour and reward him for doing it, he is likely to do it again because he enjoyed the end result.

Occasionally, punishment, a penalty inflicted for an offence, is necessary. The best type of punishment often comes from an outside source. For example, a child is told not to touch the stove because he may get burned. He disobeys and touches the stove. In doing so, he receives a burn. From that time on, he respects the heat of the stove and avoids contact with it. Therefore, a behaviour that results in an unpleasant event tends not to be repeated.

A good example of a dog learning the hard way is the dog who chases the house cat. He is told many times to leave the cat alone, yet he persists in teasing the cat. Then, one day he begins chasing the cat but the cat turns and swipes a claw across the dog's face, leaving him with a painful gash on his nose. The final result is that the dog stops chasing the cat.

TRAINING EQUIPMENT
COLLAR AND LEAD
For an Irish Setter the collar and lead that you use for training must be ones with which you are easily able to work, not too heavy for the dog and perfectly safe.

TREATS
Have a bag of treats on hand. Something nutritious and easy to swallow works best. Use a soft treat, a chunk of cheese or a piece of cooked chicken rather than a dry biscuit. By the time the dog has finished chewing a dry treat, he will forget why he is being rewarded in the first place! Using food rewards will not teach a dog to beg at the table—the only way to teach a dog to beg at the table is to give him food from the table. In training, rewarding the dog with a food treat will help him associate praise and the treats with learning new behaviours that obviously please his owner.

TRAINING BEGINS: ASK THE DOG A QUESTION
In order to teach your dog anything, you must first get his

Training with food is the preferred method with Irish Setters. They respond well to treats and praise as these gundogs want to please their masters.

attention. After all, he cannot learn anything if he is looking away from you with his mind on something else.

To get his attention, ask him, 'School?' and immediately walk over to him and give him a treat as you tell him 'Good dog.' Wait a minute or two and repeat the routine, this time with a treat in your hand as you approach within a foot of the dog. Do not go

DID YOU KNOW?
Dogs are as different from each other as people are. What works for one dog may not work for another. Have an open mind. If one method of training is unsuccessful, try another.

directly to him, but stop about a foot short of him and hold out the treat as you ask, 'School?' He will see you approaching with a treat in your hand and most likely begin walking toward you. As you meet, give him the treat and praise again.

The third time, ask the question, have a treat in your hand and walk only a short distance toward the dog so that he must walk almost all the way to you. As he reaches you, give him the treat and praise again.

By this time, the dog will probably be getting the idea that if he pays attention to you, especially when you ask that question, it will pay off in treats and enjoyable activities for him. In other words, he learns that 'school' means doing enjoyable things with you that result in treats and positive attention for him.

Remember that the dog does not understand your verbal language, he only recognises sounds. Your question translates to a series of sounds for him, and those sounds become the signal to go to you and pay attention; if he does, he will get to interact with you plus receive treats and praise.

THE BASIC COMMANDS
TEACHING SIT
Now that you have the dog's attention, attach his lead and hold it in your left hand and a food

treat in your right. Place your food hand at the dog's nose and let him lick the treat but not take it from you. Say 'Sit' and slowly raise your food hand from in front of the dog's nose up over his head so that he is looking at the ceiling. As he bends his head upward, he will have to bend his knees to

maintain his balance. As he bends his knees, he will assume a sit position. At that point, release the food treat and praise lavishly with comments such as 'Good dog! Good sit!', etc. Remember to always praise enthusiastically, because dogs relish verbal praise from their owners and feel so proud of themselves whenever they accomplish a behaviour.

You will not use food forever in getting the dog to obey your commands. Food is only used to teach new behaviours, and once the dog knows what you want when you give a specific command, you will wean him off the food treats but still maintain the verbal praise. After all, you will always have your voice with you, and there will be many times when you have no food rewards but expect the dog to obey.

TEACHING DOWN

Teaching the down exercise is easy when you understand how the dog perceives the down position, and it is very difficult when you do not. Dogs perceive the down position as a submissive

97

Praise and understanding go a long way in training the Irish Setter. Never admonish the Irish Setter too strongly or you will break his spirit.

The down command should not threaten your Irish Setter. Make sure your Irish Setter is calm before attempting to start teaching the down command.

Praise, praise, and more praise. Be patient and good things will follow.

one, therefore teaching the down exercise using a forceful method can sometimes make the dog develop such a fear of the down that he either runs away when you say 'Down' or he attempts to snap at the person who tries to force him down.

Have the dog sit close alongside your left leg, facing in the same direction as you are. Hold the lead in your left hand and a food treat in your right. Now place your left hand lightly on the top of the dog's shoulders where they meet above the spinal cord. Do not push down on the dog's shoulders; simply rest your left hand there so you can guide the dog to lie down close to your left leg rather than to swing away from your side when he drops.

Now place the food hand at the dog's nose, say 'Down' very softly (almost a whisper), and slowly lower the food hand to the dog's front feet. When the food hand reaches the floor, begin

DID YOU KNOW?

A dog in jeopardy never lies down. He stays alert on his feet because instinct tells him that he may have to run away or fight for his survival. Therefore, if a dog feels threatened or anxious, he will not lie down. Consequently, it is important to have the dog calm and relaxed as he learns the down exercise.

moving it forward along the floor in front of the dog. Keep talking softly to the dog, saying things like, 'Do you want this treat? You can do this, good dog.' Your reassuring tone of voice will help calm the dog as he tries to follow the food hand in order to get the treat.

When the dog's elbows touch the floor, release the food and praise softly. Try to get the dog to maintain that down position for several seconds before you let him sit up again. The goal here is to get the dog to settle down and not feel threatened in the down position.

TEACHING STAY

It is easy to teach the dog to stay in either a sit or a down position. Again, we use food and praise

The Irish Setter puppy is a blank canvas: what he becomes is entirely dependent on the patient, loving artist inside you.

during the teaching process as we help the dog to understand exactly what it is that we are expecting him to do.

To teach the sit/stay, start with the dog sitting on your left side as before and hold the lead in your left hand. Have a food treat in your right hand and place your food hand at the dog's nose. Say 'Stay' and step out on your right foot to stand directly in front of the dog, toe to toe, as he licks and nibbles the treat. Be sure to keep his head facing upward to maintain the sit position. Count to five and then swing around to stand next to the dog again with him on your left. As soon as you get back to the original position, release the food and praise lavishly.

> **DID YOU KNOW?**
> Occasionally, a dog and owner who have not attended formal classes have been able to earn entry-level titles by obtaining competition rules and regulations from a local kennel club and practising on their own to a degree of perfection. Obtaining the higher level titles, however, almost always requires extensive training under the tutelage of experienced instructors. In addition, the more difficult levels require more specialised equipment whereas the lower levels do not.

99

To teach the come command, approach the exercise with as little formality as possible. The Irish Setter should never sense that this is the most important command he knows.

To teach the down/stay, do the down as previously described. As soon as the dog lies down, say 'Stay' and step out on your right foot just as you did in the sit/stay. Count to five and then return to stand beside the dog with him on your left side. Release the treat and praise as always.

Within a week or ten days, you can begin to add a bit of distance between you and your dog when you leave him. When you do, use your left hand open with the palm facing the dog as a stay signal, much the same as the hand signal a police officer uses to stop traffic at an intersection. Hold the food treat in your right hand as before, but this time the food is not touching the dog's nose. He will watch the food hand

and quickly learn that he is going to get that treat as soon as you return to his side.

When you can stand 1 metre away from your dog for 30 seconds, you can then begin building time and distance in both stays. Eventually, the dog can be expected to remain in the stay position for prolonged periods of time until you return to him or call him to you. Always praise lavishly when he stays.

TEACHING COME

If you make teaching 'come' an enjoyable experience, you should never have a 'student' that does not love the game or that fails to come when called. The secret, it seems, is never to teach the word 'come.'

At times when an owner most wants his dog to come when called, the owner is likely upset or anxious and he allows these feelings to come through in the tone of his voice when he calls his dog. Hearing that desperation in his owner's voice, the dog fears the results of going to him and therefore either disobeys outright or runs in the opposite direction. The secret, therefore, is to teach the dog a game and, when you want him to come to you, simply play the game. It is practically a no-fail solution!

To begin, have several members of your family take a few food treats and each go into a

Once your Irish Setter has bonded to you, he will come to you without hesitation.

different room in the house. Take turns calling the dog, and each person should celebrate the dog's finding him with a treat and lots of happy praise. When a person calls the dog, he is actually inviting the dog to find him and get a treat as a reward for 'winning.'

A few turns of the 'Where are you?' game and the dog will realise that everyone is playing the game and that each person has a big celebration awaiting his success at locating them. Once he learns to love the game, simply calling out 'Where are you?' will bring him running from wherever he is when he hears that all-important question.

The come command is recognised as one of the most important things to teach a dog, but there are trainers who work with thousands of dogs and never teach the actual word 'Come.' Yet these dogs will race to respond to

TRAINING TIP

When calling the dog, do not say 'Come.' Say things like, 'Rover, where are you? See if you can find me! I have a biscuit for you!' Keep up a constant line of chatter with coaxing sounds and frequent questions such as, 'Where are you?' The dog will learn to follow the sound of your voice to locate you and receive his reward.

When your Irish Setter is meeting a strange dog, try not to interfere. This is part of the canine ritual, and humans can only stress the dogs. Unless you sense trouble brewing, it is not necessary to remove your dog from the encounter.

a person who uses the dog's name followed by 'Where are you?' For example, a woman has a 12-year-old companion dog who went blind, but who never fails to locate her owner when asked, 'Where are you?'

Children particularly love to play this game with their dogs. Children can hide in smaller places like a shower or bath, behind a bed or under a table. The

TRAINING TIP

Never call your dog to come to you for a correction or scold him when he reaches you. That is the quickest way to turn a 'Come' command into 'Go away fast!' Dogs think only in the present tense, and your dog will connect the scolding with coming to you, not with the misbehaviour of a few moments earlier.

An Irish Setter that is heel trained is a pleasure to walk. He will politely stay by your side without dragging you about. That is the ultimate goal of heel training.

dog needs to work a little bit harder to find these hiding places, but when he does he loves to celebrate with a treat and a tussle with a favourite youngster.

TEACHING HEEL

Heeling means that the dog walks beside the owner without pulling. It takes time and patience on the owner's part to succeed at teaching the dog that he (the owner) will not proceed unless the dog is walking calmly beside him. Pulling out ahead on the lead is definitely not acceptable.

Begin with holding the lead in your left hand as the dog sits beside your left leg. Move the loop end of the lead to your right hand but keep your left hand short on the lead so it keeps the dog in close next to you.

Say 'Heel' and step forward on your left foot. Keep the dog close to you and take three steps. Stop and have the dog sit next to

you in what we now call the 'heel position.' Praise verbally, but do not touch the dog. Hesitate a moment and begin again with 'Heel,' taking three steps and stopping, at which point the dog is told to sit again.

Your goal here is to have the dog walk those three steps without pulling on the lead. When he will walk calmly beside you for three steps without pulling, increase the number of steps you take to five. When he will walk politely beside you whilst you take five steps, you can increase the length of your walk to ten steps. Keep increasing the length of your

---

DID YOU KNOW?

Play fetch games with your puppy in an enclosed area where he can retrieve his toy and bring it back to you. Always use a toy or object designated just for this purpose. Never use a shoe, stocking or other item he may later confuse with those in your closet or underneath your chair.

TRAINING TIP

If you begin teaching the heel by taking long walks and letting the dog pull you along, he misinterprets this action as an acceptable form of taking a walk. When you pull back on the lead to counteract his pulling, he reads that tug as a signal to pull even harder!

until the dog realises that the two of you are not going anywhere until he is beside you and moving at your pace, not his. It may take some time just standing there to convince the dog that you are the leader and

TRAINING TIP

Teach your dog to HEEL in an enclosed area. Once you think the dog will obey reliably and you want to attempt advanced obedience exercises such as off-lead heeling, test him in a fenced in area so he cannot run away.

stroll until the dog will walk quietly beside you without pulling as long as you want him to heel. When you stop heeling, indicate to the dog that the exercise is over by verbally praising as you pet him and say 'OK, good dog.' The 'OK' is used as a release word meaning that the exercise is finished and the dog is free to relax.

If you are dealing with a dog who insists on pulling you around, simply 'put on your brakes' and stand your ground

you will be the one to decide on the direction and speed of your travel.

Each time the dog looks up at you or slows down to give a slack lead between the two of you, quietly praise him and say, 'Good heel. Good dog.' Eventually, the dog will begin to respond and within a few days he will be walking politely beside you without pulling on the lead. At first, the training sessions should be kept short and very positive; soon the dog will be able to walk nicely with you for increasingly longer distances. Remember also to give the dog free time and the opportunity to run and play when you have finished with heel practice.

Puppies are always waiting for your next command or word of praise. The Irish Setter is an intense and hard-working student.

103

WEANING OFF FOOD IN TRAINING

Food is used in training new behaviours. Once the dog understands what behaviour goes with a specific command, it is time to start weaning him off the food treats. At first, give a treat after each exercise. Then, start to give a treat only after every other exercise. Mix up the times when you offer a food reward and the times when you only offer praise so that the dog will never know when he is going to receive both food and praise and when he is going to receive only praise. This is

called a variable ratio reward system and it proves successful because there is always the chance that the owner will produce a treat, so the dog never stops trying for that reward. No matter what, ALWAYS give verbal praise.

OBEDIENCE CLASSES

It is a good idea to enrol in an obedience class if one is available in your area. If yours is a show dog, ringcraft classes would be more appropriate. Many areas have dog clubs that offer basic obedience training as well as preparatory classes for obedience competition. There are also local dog trainers who offer similar classes.

At obedience trials, dogs can earn titles at various levels of competition. The beginning levels of competition include basic behaviours such as sit, down, heel, etc. The more advanced levels of competition include jumping, retrieving, scent discrimination and signal work. The advanced levels require a dog and owner to put a lot of time and effort into their training and the titles that can be earned at these levels of competition are very prestigious.

OTHER ACTIVITIES FOR LIFE

Whether a dog is trained in the structured environment of a class or alone with his owner at home, there are many activities that can bring fun and rewards to both owner and dog once they have mastered basic control.

Teaching the dog to help out around the home, in the garden or on the farm provides great satisfaction to both dog and owner. In addition, the dog's help makes life a little easier for his owner and raises his stature as a valued companion to his family. It helps give the dog a purpose by occupying his mind and providing an outlet for his energy.

Backpacking is an exciting and healthy activity that the dog can be taught without assistance from more than his owner. The exercise of walking and climbing is good for man and dog alike, and the bond that they develop together is priceless.

If you are interested in participating in organised competition with your Irish Setter, there are activities other than obedience in which you and your dog can become involved. Agility is a popular and fun sport where dogs run through an obstacle course that includes various jumps, tunnels and other exercises to test the dog's speed and coordination. The owners run through the course beside their dogs to give commands and to guide them through the course. Although competitive, the focus is on fun—it's fun to do, fun to watch, and great exercise.

105

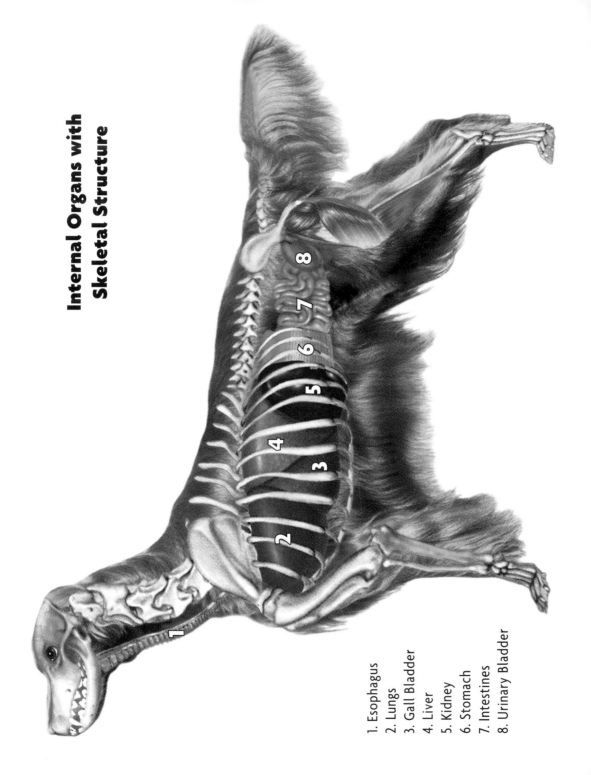

Internal Organs with Skeletal Structure

1. Esophagus
2. Lungs
3. Gall Bladder
4. Liver
5. Kidney
6. Stomach
7. Intestines
8. Urinary Bladder

HEALTH CARE OF YOUR
IRISH SETTER

Dogs suffer many of the same physical illnesses as people. They might even share many of the same psychological problems. Since people usually know more about human diseases than canine maladies, many of the terms used in this chapter will be familiar but not necessarily those used by veterinary surgeons. We will use the term *x-ray*, instead of the more acceptable term *radiograph*. We will also use the familiar term *symptoms* even though dogs don't have symptoms, which are verbal descriptions of the patient's feelings: dogs have *clinical signs*. Since dogs can't speak, we have to look for clinical signs...but we still use the term symptoms in this book.

As a general rule, medicine is practised. That term is not arbitrary. Medicine is a constantly changing art as we learn more and more about

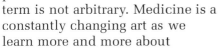

genetics, electronic aids (like CAT scans) and daily laboratory advances. There are many dog maladies, like canine hip dysplasia, which are not universally treated in the same manner. Some veterinary surgeons opt for surgery more often than others do.

SELECTING A VETERINARY SURGEON

Your selection of a veterinary surgeon should not be based upon personality (as most are) but upon their convenience to your home. You want a vet who is close because you might have emergencies or need to make multiple visits for treatments. You want a vet who has services that you might require such as tattooing and grooming facilities, as well as sophisticated pet supplies and a good reputation for ability and responsiveness. There is

Your chosen veterinary surgeon should be familiar with the latest technologies and have all the necessary equipment at his disposal.

A typical American vet's income categorised according to services provided. This survey dealt with small-animal practices.

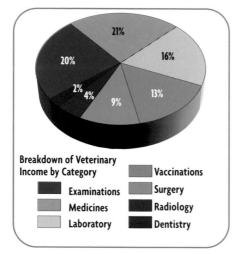

Breakdown of Veterinary Income by Category

- Examinations
- Medicines
- Laboratory
- Vaccinations
- Surgery
- Radiology
- Dentistry

dentists), eye problems (veterinary ophthalmologists), X-rays (veterinary radiologists), and surgeons who have specialities in bones, muscles or other organs. Most veterinary surgeons do routine surgery such as neutering, stitching up wounds and docking tails for those breeds in which such is required for show purposes. When the problem affecting your dog is serious, it is not unusual or impudent to get another medical opinion, although in Britain you are obliged to advise the vets concerned about this. You might also want to compare costs

nothing more frustrating than having to wait a day or more to get a response from your veterinary surgeon.

All veterinary surgeons are licensed and their diplomas and/or certificates should be displayed in their waiting rooms. There are, however, many veterinary specialities that usually require further studies and internships. There are specialists in heart problems (veterinary cardiologists), skin problems (veterinary dermatologists), teeth and gum problems (veterinary

DID YOU KNOW?
Your veterinary surgeon will probably recommend that your puppy be vaccinated before you take him outside. There are airborne diseases, parasite eggs in the grass and unexpected visits from other dogs that might be dangerous to your puppy's health.

amongst several veterinary surgeons. Sophisticated health care and veterinary services can be very costly. Don't be bashful about discussing these costs with your veterinary surgeon or his (her) staff. It is not infrequent that important decisions are based upon financial considerations.

DID YOU KNOW?
Cases of hyperactive adrenal glands (Cushing's disease) have been traced to the drinking of highly chlorinated water. Aerate or age your dog's drinking water before offering it.

First Aid at a Glance

Burns
Place the affected area under cool water; use ice if only a small area is burnt.

Bee/Insect bites
Apply ice to relieve swelling; antihistamine dosed properly.

Animal bites
Clean any bleeding area; apply pressure until bleeding subsides; go to the vet.

Spider bites
Use cold compress and a pressurised pack to inhibit venom's spreading.

Antifreeze poisoning
Immediately induce vomiting by using hydrogen peroxide.

Fish hooks
Removal best handled by vet; hook must be cut in order to remove.

Snake bites
Pack ice around bite; contact vet quickly; identify snake for proper antivenin.

Car accident
Move dog from roadway with blanket; seek veterinary aid.

Shock
Calm the dog, keep him warm; seek immediate veterinary help.

Nosebleed
Apply cold compress to the nose; apply pressure to any visible abrasion.

Bleeding
Apply pressure above the area; treat wound by applying a cotton pack.

Heat stroke
Submerge dog in cold bath; cool down with fresh air and water; go to the vet.

Frostbite/Hypothermia
Warm the dog with a warm bath, electric blankets or hot water bottles.

Abrasions
Clean the wound and wash out thoroughly with fresh water; apply antiseptic.

Remember: an injured dog may attempt to bite a helping hand from fear and confusion. Always muzzle the dog before trying to offer assistance.

109

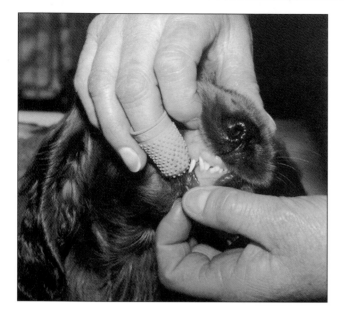

Puppies should be weaned by the time they are about two months old. A puppy that remains for at least eight weeks with its mother and litter mates usually adapts better to other dogs and people later in its life.

Some new owners have their puppy examined by a veterinary surgeon immediately, which is a good idea. Vaccination programmes usually begin when the puppy is very young.

The puppy will have its teeth examined and have its skeletal conformation and general health checked prior to certification by

Have your veterinary surgeon check the development of the puppy's teeth. Retained deciduous (baby) teeth are common in most dogs. Often these need to be removed by your vet.

PREVENTATIVE MEDICINE
It is much easier, less costly and more effective to practise preventative medicine than to fight bouts of illness and disease. Properly bred puppies come from parents that were selected based upon their genetic disease profile. Their mothers should have been vaccinated, free of all internal and external parasites, and properly nourished. For these reasons, a visit to the veterinary surgeon who cared for the dam (mother) is recommended. The dam can pass on disease resistance to her puppies, which can last for eight to ten weeks. She can also pass on parasites and many infections. That's why you should visit the veterinary surgeon who cared for the dam.

DID YOU KNOW?
Not every dog's ears are the same. Ears that are open to the air are healthier than ears

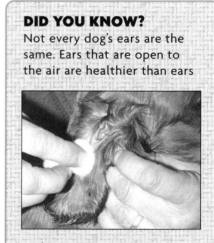

with poor air circulation. Sometimes a dog can have two differently shaped ears. You should not probe inside your dog's ears. Only clean that which is accessible with a soft cotton wipe.

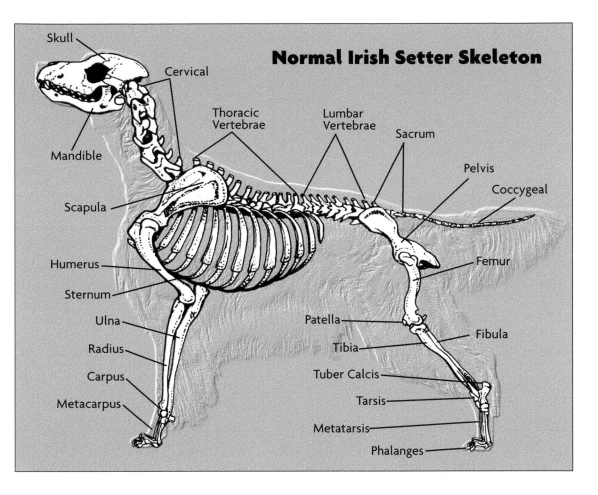

Normal Irish Setter Skeleton

Skull

Cervical

Thoracic Vertebrae

Lumbar Vertebrae

Sacrum

Pelvis

Coccygeal

Mandible

Scapula

Humerus

Sternum

Femur

Ulna

Patella

Fibula

Radius

Tibia

Carpus

Tuber Calcis

Tarsis

Metacarpus

Metatarsis

Phalanges

the veterinary surgeon. Puppies in certain breeds have problems with their kneecaps, eye cataracts and other eye problems, heart murmurs and undescended testicles. They may also have personality problems and your veterinary surgeon might have training in temperament evaluation.

VACCINATION SCHEDULING
Most vaccinations are given by injection and should only be done by a veterinary surgeon. Both he and you should keep a record of the date of the injection, the identification of the vaccine and the amount given. Some vets give a first vaccination at eight weeks, but most dog breeders prefer the course not to commence until about ten weeks because of negating any antibodies passed on by the dam. The vaccination scheduling is usually based on a two to three week cycle. You must take your vet's advice as to when

HEALTH AND VACCINATION SCHEDULE

Age in Weeks:	3RD	6TH	8TH	10TH	12TH	14TH	16TH	20-24TH
Worm Control	✔	✔	✔	✔	✔	✔	✔	✔
Neutering								✔
Heartworm*		✔						✔
Parvovirus		✔	✔					✔
Distemper			✔		✔		✔	
Hepatitis		✔			✔		✔	
Leptospirosis		✔		✔		✔		
Parainfluenza		✔		✔		✔		
Dental Examination			✔					✔
Complete Physical			✔					✔
Temperament Testing			✔					
Coronavirus					✔			
Kennel Cough		✔						
Hip Dysplasia							✔	
Rabies*								✔

Vaccinations are not instantly effective. It takes about two weeks for the dog's immunisation system to develop antibodies. Most vaccinations require annual booster shots. Your veterinary surgeon should guide you in this regard.
*Not applicable in the United Kingdom

to vaccinate as this may differ according to the vaccine used. Most vaccinations immunise your puppy against viruses.

The usual vaccines contain immunising doses of several different viruses such as distemper, parvovirus, parainfluenza and hepatitis. There are other vaccines available when the puppy is at risk. You should rely upon professional advice. This is especially true for the booster-shot programme. Most vaccination programmes require a booster when the puppy is a year old and once a year thereafter. In some cases, circumstances may require more frequent immunisations.

Kennel cough, more formally

DID YOU KNOW?

Vaccines do not work all the time. Sometimes dogs are allergic to them and many times the antibodies, which are supposed to be stimulated by the vaccine, just are not produced. You should keep your dog in the veterinary clinic for an hour after it is vaccinated to be sure there are no allergic reactions.

DID YOU KNOW?

You are your dog's caretaker and his dentist. Vets warn that plaque and tartar buildup on the teeth will damage the gums and allow bacteria to enter the dog's bloodstream, causing serious damage to the animal's vital organs. Studies show that over 50 percent of dogs have some form of gum disease before age three. Daily or weekly tooth cleaning (with a brush or soft gauze pad wipes) can add years to your dog's life.

known as tracheobronchitis, is treated with a vaccine that is sprayed into the dog's nostrils. Kennel cough is usually included in routine vaccination, but this is often not so effective as for other major diseases.

FIVE MONTHS TO ONE YEAR OF AGE
Unless you intend to breed or show your dog, neutering the puppy at six months of age is recommended. Discuss this with your veterinary surgeon.

By the time your Irish Setter is seven or eight months of age, he can be seriously evaluated for his conformation to the standard, thus determining show potential

Disease	What is it?	What causes it?	Symptoms
Leptospirosis	Severe disease that affects the internal organs; can be spread to people.	A bacterium, which is often carried by rodents, that enters through mucous membranes and spreads quickly throughout the body.	Range from fever, vomiting and loss of appetite in less severe cases to shock, irreversible kidney damage and possibly death in most severe cases.
Rabies	Potentially deadly virus that infects warm-blooded mammals. Not seen in United Kingdom.	Bite from a carrier of the virus, mainly wild animals.	1st stage: dog exhibits change in behaviour, fear. 2nd stage: dog's behaviour becomes more aggressive. 3rd stage: loss of coordination, trouble with bodily functions.
Parvovirus	Highly contagious virus, potentially deadly.	Ingestion of the virus, which is usually spread through the faeces of infected dogs.	Most common: severe diarrhoea. Also vomiting, fatigue, lack of appetite.
Kennel cough	Contagious respiratory infection.	Combination of types of bacteria and virus. Most common: *Bordetella bronchiseptica* bacteria and parainfluenza virus.	Chronic cough.
Distemper	Disease primarily affecting respiratory and nervous system.	Virus that is related to the human measles virus.	Mild symptoms such as fever, lack of appetite and mucous secretion progress to evidence of brain damage, 'hard pad.'
Hepatitis	Virus primarily affecting the liver.	Canine adenovirus type I (CAV-1). Enters system when dog breathes in particles.	Lesser symptoms include listlessness, diarrhoea, vomiting. More severe symptoms include 'blue-eye' (clumps of virus in eye).
Coronavirus	Virus resulting in digestive problems.	Virus is spread through infected dog's faeces.	Stomach upset evidenced by lack of appetite, vomiting, diarrhoea.

DID YOU KNOW?

A dental examination is in order when the dog is between six months and one year of age so any permanent teeth that have erupted incorrectly can be corrected. It is important to begin a brushing routine, preferably using a two-sided brushing technique, whereby both sides of the tooth are brushed at the same time. Durable nylon and safe edible chews should be a part of your puppy's arsenal for good health, good teeth and pleasant breath. The vast majority of dogs three to four years old and older has diseases of the gums from lack of dental attention. Using the various types of dental chews can be very effective in controlling dental plaque.

and desirability as a sire or dam. If the puppy is not top class and therefore is not a candidate for a serious breeding programme, most professionals advise neutering the puppy. Neutering has proven to be extremely beneficial to both male and female puppies. Besides eliminating the possibility of pregnancy, it inhibits (but does not prevent) breast cancer in bitches and prostate cancer in male dogs. It is very rare to diagnose breast cancer in a female dog who was spayed at or before about nine months of age before their first heat

DOGS OLDER THAN ONE YEAR
Continue to visit the veterinary surgeon at least once a year. There is no such disease as old age, but bodily functions do change with age. The eyes and ears are no longer as efficient. Liver, kidney and intestinal functions often decline. Proper dietary changes, recommended by your veterinary surgeon, can make life more pleasant for the ageing Irish Setter and you.

SKIN PROBLEMS IN IRISH SETTERS

Veterinary surgeons are consulted by dog owners for skin problems more than any other group of diseases or maladies. Dogs' skin is almost as sensitive as human skin and both suffer almost the same ailments. (Though the occurrence of acne in dogs is rare!) For this reason, veterinary dermatology has developed into a speciality practised by many veterinary surgeons.

Since many skin problems have visual symptoms that are almost identical, it requires the skill of an experienced veterinary dermatologist to identify and cure many of the more severe skin disorders. Pet shops sell many treatments for skin problems but most of the treatments are directed at symptoms and not the underlying problem(s). If your dog is suffering from a skin disorder, you should seek professional assistance as quickly as possible. As with all diseases, the earlier a problem is identified and treated, the more successful is the cure.

PARASITE BITES

Many of us are allergic to insect bites. The bites itch, erupt and may even become infected. Dogs have the same reaction to fleas, ticks and/or mites. When an insect lands on you, you have the chance to whisk it away with your hand. Unfortunately, when your dog is bitten by a flea, tick or mite, it can only scratch it away or bite it. By the time the dog has been bitten, the parasite has done some of its damage. It may also have laid eggs to cause further problems in the near future. The itching from parasite

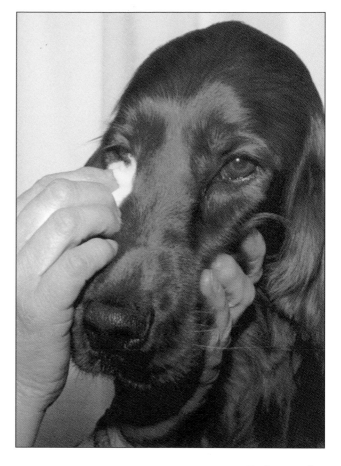

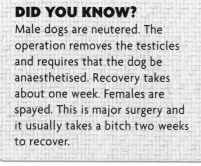

DID YOU KNOW?

Male dogs are neutered. The operation removes the testicles and requires that the dog be anaesthetised. Recovery takes about one week. Females are spayed. This is major surgery and it usually takes a bitch two weeks to recover.

bites is probably due to the saliva injected into the site when the parasite sucks the dog's blood.

AUTO-IMMUNE SKIN CONDITIONS

Auto-immune skin conditions are commonly referred to as being allergic to yourself, whilst allergies are usually inflammatory reactions to an outside stimulus. Auto-immune diseases cause serious damage to the tissues that are involved.

Tearing around the Irish Setter's eyes can indicate a significant problem. If your dog's eyes are constantly tearing, consult with your vet.

The best known auto-immune disease is lupus, which affects people as well as dogs. The symptoms are variable and may affect the kidneys, bones, blood chemistry and skin. It can be fatal to both dogs and humans, though it is not thought to be transmissible. It is usually successfully treated with cortisone, prednisone or similar corticosteroid, but extensive use of these drugs can have harmful side effects.

Allergies are fairly common in dogs, especially grass and pollen allergies. If your Irish Setter is scratching constantly after playing in the grass or inspecting your flower beds, he may be allergic to something in his environment.

ACRAL LICK GRANULOMA

Irish Setters and many other dogs have a very poorly understood syndrome called acral lick. The manifestation of the problem is the dog's tireless attack at a specific area of the body, almost always the legs. They lick so intensively that they remove the hair and skin

leaving an ugly, large wound. There is no absolute cure, but corticosteroids are the most common treatment.

AIRBORNE ALLERGIES

An interesting allergy is pollen allergy. Humans have hay fever, rose fever and other fevers with which they suffer during the pollinating season. Many dogs suffer the same allergies. When the pollen count is high, your dog might suffer but don't expect him to sneeze and have a runny nose like humans. Dogs react to pollen allergies the same way they react to fleas—they scratch and bite themselves.

Dogs, like humans, can be

develop a rash. They react in the same manner as they do to an airborne or flea allergy: they itch, scratch and bite. Thus making the diagnosis extremely difficult. Whilst pollen allergies and parasite bites are usually seasonal, food allergies are year-round problems.

FOOD INTOLERANCE

Food intolerance is the inability of the dog to completely digest certain foods. Puppies that may have done very well on their mother's milk may not do well on cow's milk. The result of this food intolerance may be loose bowels, passing gas and stomach pains. These are the only obvious symptoms of food intolerance and that makes diagnosis difficult.

TREATING FOOD PROBLEMS

It is possible to handle food allergies and food intolerance yourself. Put your dog on a diet that it has never had. Obviously if it has never eaten this new food it can't have been allergic or intolerant of it. Start with a

tested for allergens. Discuss the testing with your veterinary dermatologist.

FOOD PROBLEMS
FOOD ALLERGIES

Dogs are allergic to many foods that are best-sellers and highly recommended by breeders and veterinary surgeons. Changing the brand of food that you buy may not eliminate the problem if the element to which the dog is allergic is contained in the new brand.

Recognising a food allergy is difficult. Humans vomit or have rashes when they eat a food to which they are allergic. Dogs neither vomit nor (usually)

To prevent a dog from irritating a hot spot or granuloma, a vet may recommend an Elizabethan collar and crate rest. Hot spots can progress to much more serious problems if the dog is allowed to continue chewing at the spot. See your vet immediately for treatment.

> **DID YOU KNOW?**
> Chances are that you and your dog will have the same allergies. Your allergies are readily recognisable and usually easily treated. Your dog's allergies may be masked.

single ingredient that is not in the dog's diet at the present time. Ingredients like chopped beef or fish are common in dog's diets, so try something more exotic like rabbit, pheasant or even just vegetables. Keep the dog on this diet (with no additives) for a month. If the symptoms of food allergy or intolerance disappear,

DID YOU KNOW?

It was announced in April 1999 that the severe quarantine laws imposed on animals entering Britain from other rabies-free countries would become a thing of the past by April 2001. Rather than being confined to a kennel for six months upon arrival in Britain, animals undergo a series of blood tests and vaccinations, and are identifed by microchip implantation. Qualified pets receive a 'health passport' that allows their owners to travel with them in between Britain and other (mostly European) countries in which rabies does not exist.

Animals from countries such as the United States and Canada, where rabies is a problem, still will be subject to quarantine. Although veterinary standards are high in these countries, recently infected dogs may test negative to the disease and, without the quarantine period, may unknow-ingly introduce rabies into previously unaffected countries.

DID YOU KNOW?

Never allow your dog to swim in polluted water or public areas where water quality can be suspect. Even perfectly clear water can harbour parasites, many of which can cause serious to fatal illnesses in canines. Areas inhabited by waterfowl and other wildlife are especially dangerous.

chances are your dog has a food allergy.

Don't think that the single ingredient cured the problem. You still must find a suitable diet and ascertain which ingredient in the old diet was objectionable. This is most easily done by adding ingredients to the new diet one at a time. Let the dog stay on the modified diet for a month before you add another ingredient. Eventually, you will determine the ingredient that caused the adverse reaction.

An alternative method is to study the ingredients in the diet to which your dog is allergic or intolerant. Identify the main ingredient in this diet and eliminate the main ingredient by buying a different food that does not have that ingredient. Keep experimenting until the symptoms disappear after one month on the new diet.

A scanning electron micrograph (S. E. M.) of a dog flea, Ctenocephalides canis.

Opposite page: A scanning electron micrograph of a dog or cat flea, Ctenocephalides, magnified more than 100x. This has been colourised for effect.

EXTERNAL PARASITES

Of all the problems to which dogs are prone, none is more well known and frustrating than fleas. Flea infestation is relatively simple to cure but difficult to prevent. Parasites that are harboured

Magnified head of a dog flea, Ctenocephalides canis.

DID YOU KNOW?

Fleas have been around for millions of years and have adapted to changing host animals.

They are able to go through a complete life cycle in less than one month or they can extend their lives to almost two years by remaining as pupae or cocoons. They do not need blood or any other food for up to 20 months.

They have been measured as being able to jump 300,000 times and can jump 150 times their length in any direction including straight up. Those are just a few of the reasons they are so successful in infesting a dog!

inside the body are a bit more difficult to eradicate but they are easier to control.

FLEAS

To control a flea infestation you have to understand the flea's life cycle. Fleas are often thought of as a summertime problem but centrally heated homes have changed the patterns and fleas can be found at any time of the year. The most effective method of flea control is a two-stage approach: one stage to kill the adult fleas, and the other to control the development of pre-adult fleas. Unfortunately, no single active ingredient is effective against all stages of the life cycle.

LIFE CYCLE STAGES

During its life, a flea will pass through four life stages: egg, larva, pupa and adult. The adult stage is the most visible and irritating stage of the flea life

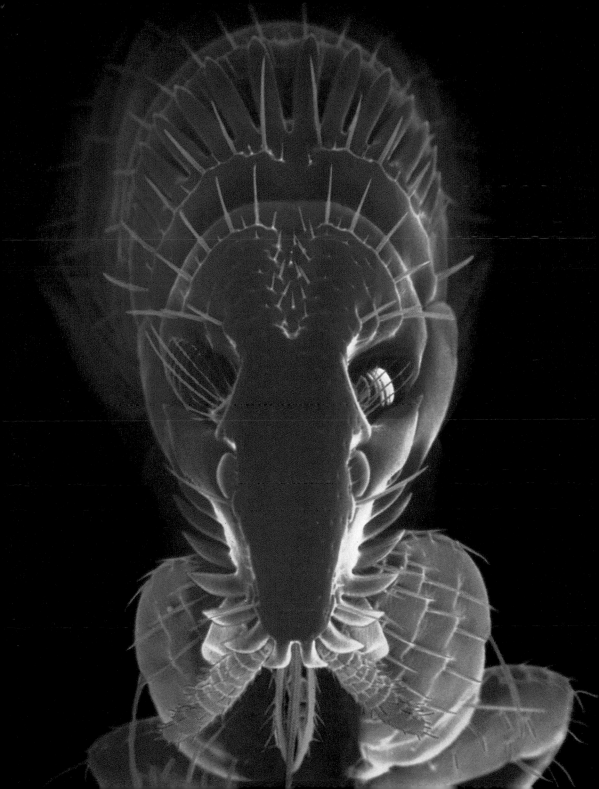

The Life Cycle of the Flea

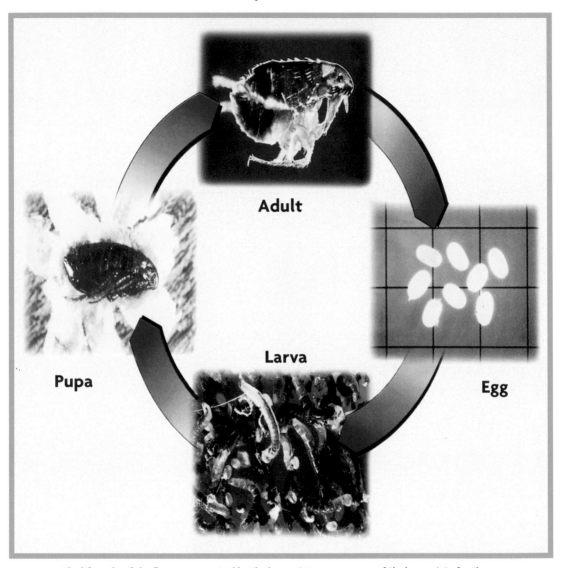

Adult

Pupa

Larva

Egg

The life cycle of the flea was posterised by Fleabusters®. Poster courtesy of Fleabusters®, R_x for Fleas.

cycle and this is why the majority of flea-control products concentrate on this stage. The fact is that adult fleas account for only 1% of the total flea population, and the other 99% exist in pre-adult stages, i.e., eggs, larvae and pupae. The pre-adult stages are barely visible to the naked eye.

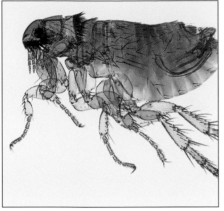

PHOTO BY JEAN CLAUDE REVY/PHOTOTAKE.

THE LIFE CYCLE OF THE FLEA
Eggs are laid on the dog, usually in quantities of about 20 or 30, several times a day. The female adult flea must have a blood meal before each egg-laying session. When first laid, the eggs will cling to the dog's fur, as the eggs are still moist. However, they will quickly dry out and fall from the dog, especially if the dog moves around or scratches. Many eggs will fall off in the dog's favourite area or an area in which

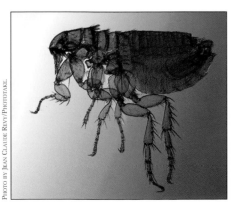

PHOTO BY JEAN CLAUDE REVY/PHOTOTAKE.

ON GUARD: CATCHING FLEAS OFF GUARD

Consider the following ways to arm yourself against fleas:
• Add a small amount of pennyroyal or eucalyptus oil to your dog's bath. These natural remedies repel fleas.
• Supplement your dog's food with fresh garlic (minced or grated) and a hearty amount of brewer's yeast, both of which ward off fleas.
• Use a flea comb on your dog daily. Submerge fleas in a cup of bleach to kill them quickly.
• Confine the dog to only a few rooms to limit the spread of fleas in the home.
• Vacuum daily...and get all of the crevices! Dispose of the bag every few days until the problem is under control.
• Wash your dog's bedding daily. Cover cushions where your dog sleeps with towels, and wash the towels often.

A male dog flea, *Ctenocephalides canis*.

The eggs of the dog flea.

Male cat fleas, *Ctenocephalides felis*, are very commonly found on dogs.

he spends a lot of time, such as his bed.

Once the eggs fall from the dog onto the carpet or furniture, they will hatch into larvae. This takes from one to ten days. Larvae are not particularly mobile, and will usually travel only a few inches from where they hatch. However, they do have a tendency to move away from light and heavy traffic—under furniture and behind doors are common places to find high quantities of flea larvae.

The flea larvae feed on dead organic matter, including adult flea faeces, until they are ready to change into adult fleas. Fleas will usually remain as larvae for around seven days. After this period, the larvae will pupate into protective pupae. While inside the pupae, the larvae will undergo metamorphosis and change into

PHOTO BY DWIGHT R KUHN.

adult fleas. This can take as little time as a few days, but the adult fleas can remain inside the pupae waiting to hatch for up to two years. The pupae are signalled to hatch by certain stimuli, such as physical pressure—the pupae's being stepped on, heat from an animal lying on the pupae or increased carbon dioxide levels and vibrations—indicating that a suitable host is available.

Once hatched, the adult flea must feed within a few days. Once the adult flea finds a host, it will not leave voluntarily. It only becomes dislodged by grooming or the host animal's scratching. The adult flea will remain on the host for the duration of its life unless forcibly removed.

TREATING THE ENVIRONMENT AND THE DOG

Treating fleas should be a two-pronged attack. First, the environment needs to be treated; this includes carpets and furniture,

PHOTO BY DWIGHT R KUHN.

DID YOU KNOW?

Never mix flea control products without first consulting your veterinary surgeon. Some products can become toxic when combined with others and can cause serious or fatal consequences.

especially the dog's bedding and areas underneath furniture. The environment should be treated with a household spray containing an Insect Growth Regulator (IGR) and an insecticide to kill the adult fleas. Most IGRs are effective against eggs and larvae; they actually mimic the fleas' own hormones and stop the eggs and larvae from developing into adult fleas. There are currently no treatments available to attack the pupa stage of the life cycle, so the adult insecticide is used to kill the newly hatched adult fleas before they find a host. Most IGRs are active for many months, whilst adult insecticides are only active for a few days.

When treating with a household spray, it is a good idea to vacuum before applying the product. This stimulates as many pupae as possible to hatch into adult fleas. The vacuum cleaner should also be treated with a flea treatment to prevent the eggs and larvae that have been hoovered into the vacuum bag from hatching.

The second stage of treatment is to apply an adult insecticide to the dog. Traditionally, this would be in the form of a collar or a spray, but more recent innovations include digestible insecticides that poison the fleas when they ingest the dog's blood. Alternatively, there are drops that, when placed on the back of the animal's neck, spread throughout the fur and skin to kill adult fleas.

DID YOU KNOW?

Two types of products should be used when treating fleas—a product to treat the pet and a product to treat the home. Adult fleas represent less than 1% of the flea population. The pre-adult fleas (eggs, larvae and pupae) represent more than 99% of the flea population and are found in the environment; it is in the case of pre-adult fleas that products containing an Insect Growth Regulator (IGR) should be used in the home.

IGRs are a new class of compounds used to prevent the development of insects. They do not kill the insect outright, but instead use the insect's biology against it to stop it from completing its growth. Products that contain methoprene are the world's first and leading IGRs. Used to control fleas and other insects, this type of IGR will stop flea larvae from developing and protect the house for up to seven months.

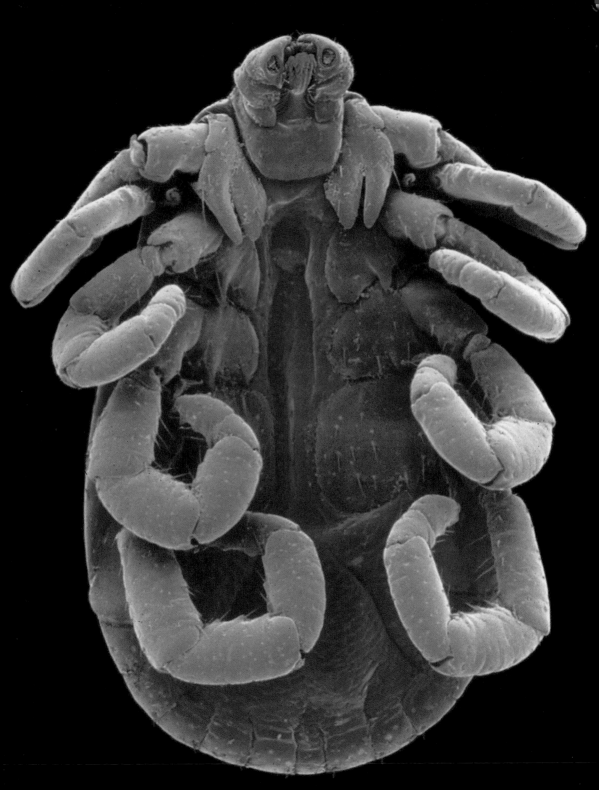

TICKS AND MITES

Though not as common as fleas, ticks and mites are found all over the tropical and temperate world. They don't bite, like fleas; they harpoon. They dig their sharp proboscis (nose) into the dog's skin and drink the blood. Their only food and drink is dog's blood. Dogs can get Lyme disease, Rocky Mountain spotted fever (normally found in the USA only), paralysis and many other diseases from ticks and mites. They may live where fleas are found and they like to hide in cracks or seams in walls wherever dogs live. They are controlled the same way fleas are controlled.

The dog tick, *Dermacentor variabilis*, may well be the most common dog tick in many geographical areas, especially those areas where the climate is hot and humid.

PHOTO BY JEAN CLAUDE REVY/PHOTOTAKE

An uncommon dog tick of the genus *Ixode*. Magnified 10x.

Opposite page: The dog tick, *Dermacentor variabilis*, is probably the most common tick found on dogs. Look at the strength in its eight legs! No wonder it's hard to detach them.

Most dog ticks have life expectancies of a week to six months, depending upon climatic conditions. They can neither jump nor fly, but they can crawl slowly and can range up to 5 metres (16 feet) to reach a sleeping or unsuspecting dog.

MANGE

Mites cause a skin irritation called mange. Some are contagious, like *Cheyletiella*, ear mites, scabies and chiggers. The non-contagious mites are *Demodex*. Mites that cause ear-mite infestation are usually controlled with ivermectin, which is often toxic to Collies and probably should be avoided in all herding breeds.

It is essential that your dog be treated for mange as quickly as possible because some forms of mange are transmissible to people.

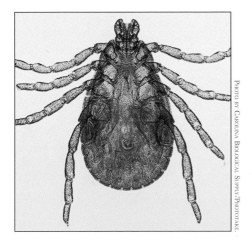

PHOTO BY CAROLINA BIOLOGICAL SUPPLY/PHOTOTAKE

A brown dog tick, *Rhipicephalus sanguineus*, is an uncommon but annoying tick found on dogs.

127

Two views of the mange mite, *Psoroptes bovis.*

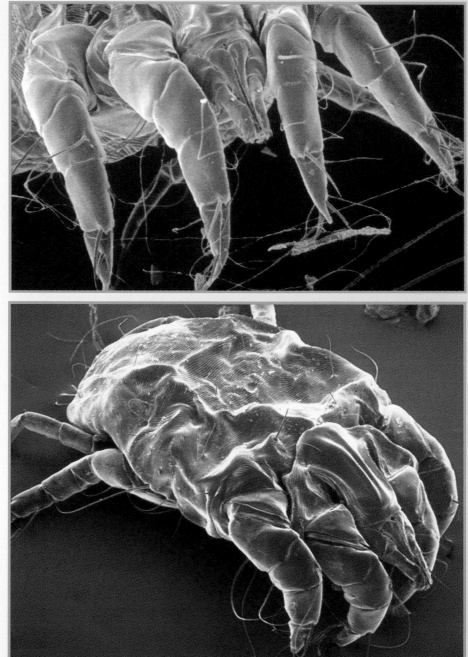

INTERNAL PARASITES

Most animals—fishes, birds and mammals, including dogs and humans—have worms and other parasites that live inside their bodies. According to Dr Herbert R Axelrod, the fish pathologist, there are two kinds of parasites: dumb and smart. The smart parasites live in peaceful coopera-tion with their hosts (symbiosis), while the dumb parasites kill their host. Most of the worm infections are relatively easy to control. If they are not controlled they eventually weaken the host dog to the point that other medical problems occur, but they are not dumb parasites.

ROUNDWORMS

The roundworms that infect dogs are scientifically known as *Toxocara canis*. They live in the dog's intestine. The worms shed eggs continually. It has been estimated that a dog produces about 150 grammes of faeces every day. Each gramme of faeces averages 10,000–12,000 eggs of roundworms. There are no known areas in which dogs roam that do not contain roundworm eggs. The greatest danger of roundworms is

DID YOU KNOW?

Ridding your puppy of worms is VERY IMPORTANT because certain worms that puppies carry, such as tapeworms and roundworms, can infect humans.

Breeders initiate a deworming programme at or about four weeks of age. The routine is repeated every two or three weeks until the puppy is three months old. The breeder from whom you obtained your puppy should provide you with the complete details of the deworming programme.

Your veterinary surgeon can prescribe and monitor the programme of deworming for you. The usual programme is treating the puppy every 15–20 days until the puppy is positively worm free.

It is not advised that you treat your puppy with drugs that are not recommended professionally.

The roundworm, *Rhabditis*. The roundworm can infect both dogs and humans.

129

The roundworm *Rhabditis*.

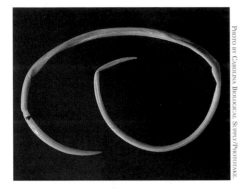

Photo by Carolina Biological Supply/Phototake.

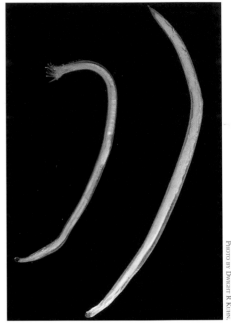

Photo by Dwight R Kuhn.

Male and female hookworms, *Ancylostoma caninum*, are uncommonly found in pet or show dogs in Britain. Hookworms may infect other dogs that have exposure to grasslands.

that they infect people too! It is wise to have your dog tested regularly for roundworms.

Pigs also have roundworm infections that can be passed to humans and dogs. The typical roundworm parasite is called *Ascaris lumbricoides*.

HOOKWORMS

The worm *Ancylostoma caninum* is commonly called the dog hookworm. It is dangerous to humans and cats. It also has teeth

by which it attaches itself to the intestines of the dog. It changes the site of its attachment about six times a day and the dog loses blood from each detachment, possibly causing iron-deficiency anaemia. Hookworms are easily purged from the dog with many medications. Milbemycin oxime, which also serves as a heartworm preventative in Collies, can be used for this purpose.

In Britain the 'temperate climate' hookworm (*Uncinaria stenocephala*) is rarely found in pet or show dogs, but can occur in hunting packs, racing Greyhounds and sheepdogs because the worms can be prevalent wherever dogs are exercised regularly on grassland.

DID YOU KNOW?

Caring for the puppy starts before the puppy is born by keeping the dam healthy and well-nourished. Most puppies have worms, even if they are not evident, so a worming programme is essential. The worms continually shed eggs except during their dormant stage, when they just rest in the tissues of the puppy. During this stage they are not evident during a routine examination.

Average size dogs can pass 1,360,000 roundworm eggs every day.

For example, if there were only 1 million dogs in the world, the world would be saturated with 1,300 metric tonnes of dog faeces.

These faeces would contain 15,000,000,000 roundworm eggs.

7–31% of home gardens and children's play boxes in the U. S. contain roundworm eggs.

Flushing dog's faeces down the toilet is not a safe practice because the usual sewage treatments do not destroy roundworm eggs.

Infected puppies start shedding roundworm eggs at 3 weeks of age. They can be infected by their mother's milk.

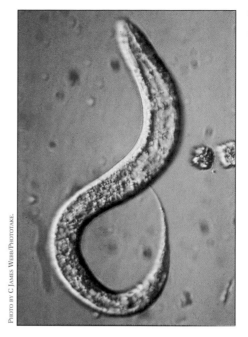

The infective stage of the hookworm larva.

PHOTO BY C. JAMES WEBB/PHOTOTAKE.

TAPEWORMS

There are many species of tapeworms. They are carried by fleas! The dog eats the flea and starts the tapeworm cycle. Humans can also be infected with tapeworms, so don't eat fleas! Fleas are so small that your dog could pass them onto your hands, your plate or your food and thus make it possible for you to ingest a flea which is carrying tapeworm eggs.

While tapeworm infection is not life threatening in dogs (smart parasite!), it can be the cause of a very serious liver disease for humans. About 50 percent of the humans infected with

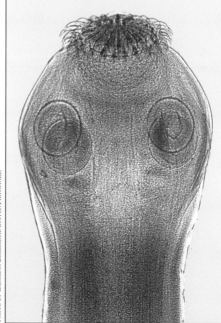

The head and rostellum (the round prominence on the scolex) of a tapeworm, which infects dogs and humans.

PHOTO BY CAROLINA BIOLOGICAL SUPPLY/PHOTOTAKE.

131

Echinococcus multilocularis, a type of tapeworm that causes alveolar hydatis, perish.

HEARTWORMS

Heartworms are thin, extended worms up to 30 cms (12 ins) long which live in a dog's heart and the major blood vessels surrounding it. Dogs may have up to 200 of these worms. The symptoms may be loss of energy, loss of appetite, coughing, the development of a pot belly and anaemia.

Heartworms are transmitted by mosquitoes. The mosquito drinks the blood of an infected dog and takes in larvae with the blood. The larvae, called microfilaria, develop within the body of the mosquito and are passed on to the next dog bitten after the larvae mature. It takes two to three weeks for the larvae to develop to the infective stage within the body of the mosquito. Dogs should be treated at about six weeks of age, then every six months.

DID YOU KNOW?

Humans, rats, squirrels, foxes, coyotes, wolves, mixed breeds of dogs and purebred dogs are all susceptible to tapeworm infection. Except in humans, tapeworms are usually not a fatal infection.

Infected individuals can harbour a thousand parasitic worms.

Tapeworms have two sexes—male and female (many other worms have only one sex—male and female in the same worm).

If dogs eat infected rats or mice, they get the tapeworm disease.

One month after attaching to a dog's intestine, the worm starts shedding eggs. These eggs are infective immediately.

Infective eggs can live for a few months without a host animal.

Roundworms, whipworms and tapeworms are just a few of the other commonly known worms that infect dogs.

Blood testing for heartworms is not necessarily indicative of how seriously your dog is infected. This is a dangerous disease. Although heartworm is a problem for dogs in America, Australia, Asia and Central Europe, dogs in the United Kingdom are not affected by heartworm.

The heartworm, *Dirofilaria immitis*.

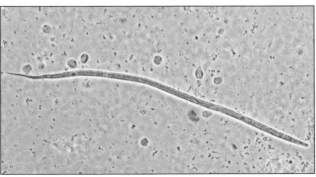

Photo by James E Hayden, RPB/Phototake

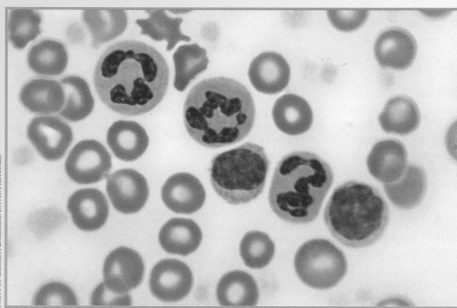

Magnified heartworm larvae, *Dirofilaria immitis.*

The heart of a dog infected with canine heartworm, *Dirofilaria immitis.*

133

CDS: COGNITIVE DYSFUNCTION SYNDROME
'Old Dog Syndrome'

There are many ways for you to evaluate old-dog syndrome. Veterinary surgeons have defined CDS (cognitive dysfunction syndrome) as the gradual deterioration of cognitive abilities. These are indicated by changes in the dog's behaviour. When a dog changes its routine response, and maladies have been eliminated as the cause of these behavioural changes, then CDS is the usual diagnosis.

More than half the dogs over 8 years old suffer some form of CDS. The older the dog, the more chance it has of suffering from CDS. In humans, doctors often dismiss the CDS behavioural changes as part of 'winding down.'

There are four major signs of CDS: frequent toilet accidents inside the home, sleeps much more or much less than normal, acts confused, and fails to respond to social stimuli.

SYMPTOMS OF CDS

FREQUENT TOILET ACCIDENTS
- *Urinates in the house.*
- *Defecates in the house.*
- *Doesn't signal that he wants to go out.*

SLEEP PATTERNS
- *Moves much more slowly.*
- *Sleeps more than normal during the day.*
- *Sleeps less during the night.*
- *Walks around listlessly and without a destination goal.*

CONFUSION
- *Goes outside and just stands there.*
- *Appears confused with a faraway look in his eyes.*
- *Hides more often.*
- *Doesn't recognise friends.*
- *Doesn't come when called.*

FAILS TO RESPOND TO SOCIAL STIMULI
- *Comes to people less frequently, whether called or not.*
- *Doesn't tolerate petting for more than a short time.*
- *Doesn't come to the door when you return home from work.*

IRISH SETTER

The term old is a qualitative term. For dogs, as well as their masters, old is relative. Certainly we can all distinguish between an Irish Setter puppy and an adult Irish Setter—there are the obvious physical traits, such as size, appearance and facial expressions, and personality traits. Puppies and young dogs like to play with children. Children's natural exuberance is a good match for the seemingly endless energy of young dogs. They like to run, jump, chase and retrieve. When dogs grow up and cease their interaction with children, they are often thought of as being too old to play with the kids.

On the other hand, if an Irish Setter is only exposed to people over 60 years of age, its life will normally be less active and it will not seem to be getting old as its activity level slows down.

If people live to be 100 years old, dogs live to be 20 years old. Whilst this is a good rule of thumb, it is very inaccurate. When trying to compare dog years to human years, you cannot make a generalisation about all dogs. You can make the generalisation that, 11–12 years is a good life

span for an Irish Setter, which is quite good compared to many other purebred dogs that may only live to 8 or 9 years of age. Some Irish Setters have been known to live to 15 years. Dogs are generally considered mature within three years, but they can reproduce even earlier. So the first three years of a dog's life are like seven times that of comparable humans. That means a 3-year-old dog is like a 21-year-old human. As the curve of comparison shows, there is no hard and fast rule for comparing dog and human ages. The comparison is

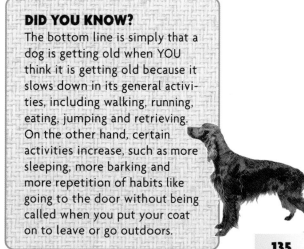

DID YOU KNOW?
The bottom line is simply that a dog is getting old when YOU think it is getting old because it slows down in its general activities, including walking, running, eating, jumping and retrieving. On the other hand, certain activities increase, such as more sleeping, more barking and more repetition of habits like going to the door without being called when you put your coat on to leave or go outdoors.

Treat your senior Irish Setter with the respect and care that you would a grandparent. For the years of devotion and friendship, the older dog deserves very special consideration.

implement certain therapeutic and preventive medical strategies with the help of their veterinary surgeons. A senior-care programme should include at least two veterinary visits per year, screening sessions to determine the dog's health status, as well as nutritional counselling. Veterinary surgeons determine the senior dog's health status through a blood smear for a complete blood count, serum chemistry made even more difficult, for not all humans age at the same rate...and human females live longer than human males.

WHAT TO LOOK FOR IN SENIORS

Most veterinary surgeons and behaviourists use the seventh year mark as the time to consider a dog a 'senior.' The term 'senior' does not imply that the dog is geriatric and has begun to fail in mind and body. Ageing is essentially a slowing process. Humans readily admit that they feel a difference in their activity level from age 20 to 30, and then from 30 to 40, etc. By treating the seven-year-old dog as a senior, owners are able to

profile with electrolytes, urinalysis, blood pressure check, electrocardiogram, ocular tonometry (pressure on the eyeball), and dental prophylaxis.

Such an extensive programme for senior dogs is well advised before owners start to see the obvious physical signs of ageing, such as slower and inhibited movement, greying, increased sleep/nap periods, and disinterest in play and other activity. This

DID YOU KNOW?

The symptoms listed below are symptoms that gradually appear and become more noticeable. They are not life threatening; however, the symptoms below are to be taken very seriously and a discussion with your veterinary surgeon is warranted:

• Your dog cries and whimpers when it moves and stops running completely.

• Convulsions start or become more serious and frequent. The usual convulsion (spasm) is when the dog stiffens and starts to tremble being unable or unwilling to move. The seizure usually lasts for 5 to 30 minutes.

• Your dog drinks more water and urinates more frequently. Wetting and bowel accidents take place indoors without warning.

• Vomiting becomes more and more frequent.

preventative programme promises a longer, healthier life for the ageing dog. Amongst the physical problems common in ageing dogs are the loss of sight and hearing, arthritis, kidney and liver failure, diabetes mellitus, heart disease, and Cushing's disease (a hormonal disease).

In addition to the physical manifestations discussed, there are some behavioural changes and problems related to ageing dogs.

Dogs suffering from hearing or vision loss, dental discomfort or arthritis can become aggressive. Likewise the near-deaf and/or blind dog may be startled more easily and react in an unexpectedly aggressive manner. Seniors suffering from senility can become more impatient and irritable. Housesoiling accidents are associated with loss of mobility, kidney problems, loss of sphincter control as well as plaque accumulation, physiological brain changes, and reactions to medications. Older dogs, just like young puppies, suffer from separation anxiety, which can lead to excessive barking, whining, housesoiling, and destructive behaviour. Seniors may become fearful of everyday sounds, such as vacuum cleaners, heaters, thunder, and passing traffic. Some dogs have difficulty sleeping, due to discomfort, the need for frequent toilet visits, and the like.

Owners should avoid spoiling the older dog with too many fatty treats. Obesity is a common problem in older dogs and subtracts years from their lifespan. Keep the senior dog as trim as possible since excessive weight puts additional stress on the body's vital organs. Some breeders recommend supplementing the diet with foods high in fibre and

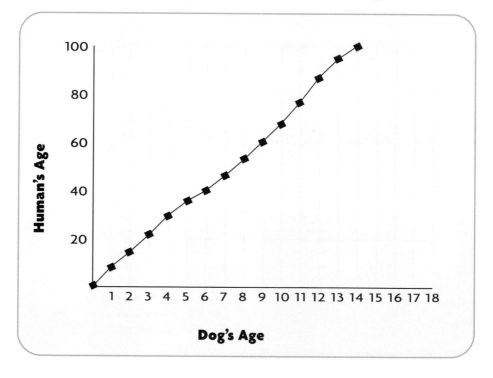

lower in calories. Adding fresh vegetables and marrow broth to the senior's diet makes a tasty, low-calorie, low-fat supplement. Vets also offer speciality diets for senior dogs that are worth exploring.

Senior Irish Setters slow down and will not welcome exercise sessions as readily as puppies and adults. Let your senior take it easy as he sees fit, but don't let him sleep all day.

Your dog, as he nears his twilight years, needs his owner's patience and good care more than ever. Never punish an older dog for an accident or abnormal behaviour. For all the years of love, protection and companionship that your dog has provided, he deserves special attention and courtesies. The older dog may need to relieve himself at 3 a.m. because he can no longer hold it for eight hours. Older dogs may not be able to remain crated for more than two or three hours. It may be time to give up a sofa or chair to your old friend. Although he may not seem as enthusiastic about your attention and petting, he does appreciate the considerations you offer as he gets older.

Your Irish Setter does not understand why his world is slowing down. Owners must make the transition into the golden years as pleasant and rewarding as possible.

WHAT TO DO WHEN THE TIME COMES

You are never fully prepared to make a rational decision about putting your dog to sleep. It is very obvious that you love your Irish Setter or you would not be reading this book. Putting a loved dog to sleep is extremely difficult. It is a decision that must be made with your veterinary surgeon. You are usually forced to make the decision when one of the life-threatening symptoms listed above becomes serious enough for you to seek medical (veterinary) help.

If the prognosis of the malady indicates the end is near and your beloved pet will only suffer more and experience no enjoyment for the balance of its life, then euthanasia is the right choice.

WHAT IS EUTHANASIA?

Euthanasia derives from the Greek meaning *good death*. In other words, it means the planned, painless killing of a dog suffering from a painful, incurable condition, or who is so aged that it cannot walk, see, eat or control its excretory functions.

Euthanasia is usually accomplished by injection with an overdose of an anaesthesia or barbiturate. Aside from the prick of the needle, the experience is usually painless.

HOW ABOUT YOU?

The decision to euthanise your dog is never easy. The days during which the dog becomes ill and the end occurs can be unusually stressful for you. If this is your first experience with the death of a loved one, you may need the comfort dictated by your religious beliefs. If you are the head of the family and have children, you should have involved them in the decision of putting your Irish Setter to sleep. Usually your dog can be maintained on drugs for a few days in order to give you ample time to make a decision. During this time, talking with members of your family or even people who have lived through this same experience can ease the burden of your inevitable decision.

THE FINAL RESTING PLACE

Dogs can have some of the same privileges as humans. They can occasionally be buried in a pet cemetery which is generally expensive, or if they have died at home can buried in your garden in a place suitably marked with some stone or newly planted tree or bush. Alternatively they can be cremated and the ashes returned to you, or some people prefer to leave their dogs at the surgery for the vet to dispose of.

All of these options should be discussed frankly and openly with your veterinary surgeon. Do not be afraid to ask financial questions. Cremations can be individual, but a less expensive option is mass cremation, although of course the ashes can not then be returned. Vets can usually arrange cremation services on your behalf, but you must be aware that in Britain if your dog has died at the surgery the vet cannot legally allow you to take your dog's body home.

DID YOU KNOW?

Euthanasia must be done by a licensed veterinary surgeon. There also may be societies for the prevention of cruelty to animals in your area. They often offer this service upon a vet's recommendation.

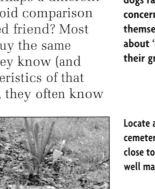

usually be housetrained and will have an already developed personality. In this case, you can find out if you like each other after a few hours of being together.

The decision is, of course, your own. Do you want another Irish Setter or perhaps a different breed so as to avoid comparison with your beloved friend? Most people usually buy the same breed because they know (and love) the characteristics of that breed. Then, too, they often know

The greying muzzle and face of this old fellow shows his many years of dedication and experience. Unlike humans, dogs rarely concern themselves about 'hiding their grey.'

GETTING ANOTHER DOG?

The grief of losing your beloved dog will be as lasting as the grief of losing a human friend or relative. In most cases, if your dog died of old age (if there is such a thing), it had slowed down considerably. Do you want a new Irish Setter puppy to replace it? Or are you better off in finding a more mature Irish Setter, say two to three years of age, which will

Locate a pet cemetery that is close to home and well maintained.

people who have the same breed and perhaps they are lucky enough that a breeder they know and respect expects a litter soon. What could be better?

Many pet cemeteries have facilities for storing the cremains of your dog.

DID YOU KNOW?
The more open discussion you have about the whole stressful occurrence, the easier it will be for you when the time comes.

IRISH SETTER

When you purchased your Irish Setter you should have made it clear to the breeder whether you wanted one just as a loveable companion and pet, or if you hoped to be buying an Irish Setter with show prospects. No reputable breeder would have sold you a young puppy saying that it was definitely of show quality for so much can go wrong during the early weeks and months of a puppy's development. If you plan to show, what you will hopefully have acquired is a puppy with 'show potential.'

To the novice, exhibiting an Irish Setter in the show ring may look easy but it usually takes a lot of hard work and devotion to do top winning at a show such as the prestigious Crufts, not to mention a little luck too!

The first concept that the canine novice learns when watching a dog show is that each dog first competes against members of its own breed. Once the judge has selected the best member of each breed, provided that the show is judged on a Group system, that chosen dog will compete with other dogs in its group. Finally the best of each group will compete for Best in Show and Reserve Best in Show.

The second concept that you must understand is that the dogs are not actually competing against one another. The judge compares each dog against the breed standard, which is a written description of the ideal specimen of the breed. Whilst some early breed standards were indeed based on specific dogs that were famous or popular, many dedicated enthusiasts say that a perfect specimen, described in the standard, has never been bred. Thus the 'perfect' dog never walked into a show ring, has never been bred and, to the woe of dog breeders around the globe, does not exist. Breeders attempt to get as close to this ideal as possible, with every litter, but theoretically the 'perfect' dog is so elusive that it is impossible. (And

DID YOU KNOW?

The Kennel Club divides its dogs into seven Groups: Gundogs, Utility, Working, Toy, Terrier, Hounds and Pastoral.*

*The Pastoral Group, established in 1999, includes those sheepdog breeds previously categorised in the Working Group.

Beauty and brains to perfection: winning the title of Supreme Champion of Crufts in 1995 is Sh Ch Starchelle Chicago Bear. The Irish Setter won this title three times in the 1990s, more than any other breed.

if the 'perfect' dog were born, breeders and judges would never agree that it was indeed 'perfect.')

If you are interested in exploring dog shows, your best bet is to join your local breed club. These clubs often host both Championship and Open Shows, and sometimes Match meetings and Special Events, all of which could be of interest, even if you are only an onlooker. Clubs also send out newsletters and some organise training days and seminars in order that people may

WINNING THE TICKET
Earning a championship at Kennel Club shows is the most difficult in the world. Compared to the United States and Canada where it is relatively not 'challenging,' collecting three green tickets not only requires much time and effort, it can be very expensive! Challenge Certificates, as the tickets are properly known, are the building blocks of champions—good breeding, good handling, good training and good luck!

143

Winning Best in Group at the 1999 Crufts Dog Show is Sh Ch Caspians Intrepid.

learn more about their chosen breed. To locate the nearest breed club for you, contact The Kennel Club, the ruling body for the British dog world. The Kennel Club governs not only conformation shows but also working trials, obedience trials, agility trials and field trials. The Kennel Club furnishes the rules and regulations for all these events plus general dog registration and other basic requirements of dog ownership. Its annual show called

Winning Best in Group at the 1999 Crufts Dog Show is Sh Ch Caspians Intrepid.

The third Irish Setter to take home this trophy in the 1990s, here's Sh Ch Caspians Intrepid sitting with his thrilled handler.

Winning with your own Irish Setter is an unmistakable joy. Dog showing requires patience and experience, but it all pays off grandly for both dog and handler.

the Crufts Dogs Show, held in Birmingham, is the largest bench show in England. Every year over 20,000 of the U.K.'s best dogs qualify to participate in this marvellous show which lasts four days.

The Kennel Club governs many different kinds of shows in Great Britain, Australia, South Africa and beyond. At the most competitive and prestigious of these shows, the Championship Shows, a dog can earn Challenge Certificates, and thereby become a Show Champion or a Champion. A dog must earn three Challenge Certificates under three different judges to earn the prefix of 'Sh Ch' or 'Ch'. Note Irish Setters must also qualify in a field trial in

CLASSES AT DOG SHOWS
There can be as many as 18 classes per sex for your breed. Check the show schedule carefully to make sure that you have entered your dog in the appropriate class. Among the classes offered can be: Beginners; Minor Puppy (ages 6 to 9 months); Puppy (ages 6 to 12 months); Junior (ages 6 to 18 months); Beginners (handler or dog never won first place) as well as the following, each of which is defined in the schedule: Maiden; Novice; Tyro; Debutant; Undergraduate; Graduate; Postgraduate; Minor Limit; Mid Limit; Limit; Open; Veteran; Stud Dog; Brood Bitch; Progeny; Brace and Team.

HOW TO ENTER A DOG SHOW

1. Obtain an entry form and show schedule from the Show Secretary.
2. Select the classes that you want to enter and complete the entry form.
3. Transfer your dog into your name at The Kennel Club. (Be sure that this matter is handled before entering.)
4. Find out how far in advance show entries must be made. Oftentimes it's more than a couple of months.

order to gain the title of full champion. Challenge Certificates are awarded to a very small percentage of the dogs competing, especially as dogs that are already Champions compete with others for these coveted CCs. The number of Challenge Certificates awarded in any one year is based upon the total number of dogs in each breed entered for competition. There are three types of Championship Shows: an all-breed General Championship show for all Kennel-Club-recognised breeds; a Group Championship Show, limited to

Once the competition is over, the winners are always the best dog folk to meet. Invariably, they are always in the best mood. Although winning isn't everything, in conformation shows, it sure makes the ride home more exhilarating.

Each Irish Setter entered is 'stacked up' against the breed standard. Performance, by dog as well as the handler, also plays a significant part in the judge's evaluation: it's not called a dog show for nothing.

breeds within one of the groups; and a Breed Show, usually confined to a single breed. The Kennel Club determines which breeds at which Championship Shows will have the opportunity to earn Challenge Certificates (or tickets). Serious exhibitors often will opt not to participate if the tickets are withheld at a particular show. This policy makes earning championships ever more difficult to accomplish.

Open Shows are generally less competitive and are frequently used as 'practice shows' for young dogs. There are hundreds of Open Shows each year that can be invitingly social events and are great first show experiences for the novice. Even

DID YOU KNOW?

You can get information about dog shows from kennel clubs and breed clubs:

Fédération Cynologique Internationale
14, rue Leopold II, B-6530 Thuin, Belgium
www.fci.be

The Kennel Club
1-5 Clarges St., Piccadilly, London W1Y
8AB, UK
www.the-kennel-club.org.uk

American Kennel Club
5580 Centerview Dr., Raleigh, NC 27606-
3390, USA
www.akc.org

Canadian Kennel Club
89 Skyway Ave., Suite 100, Etobicoke,
Ontario
M9W 6R4 Canada
www.ckc.ca

147

if you're considering just watching a show to wet your paws, an Open Show is a great choice.

Whilst Championship and Open Shows are most important for the beginner to understand, there are other types of shows in which the interested dog owner can participate. Training clubs sponsor Matches that can be entered on the day of the show for a nominal fee. In these introductory-level exhibitions, two dogs

A bench show requires that the dogs remain 'on the benches' for the duration of the showing. Is there any doubt that crate training a show dog pays off during a dog show. These Irish Setters seem to be enjoying their naps.

are pulled out of a hat and 'matched,' the winner of that match goes on to the next round, and eventually only one dog is left undefeated.

Exemption Shows are much more light-hearted affairs with usually only four pedigree classes and several 'fun' classes, all of which can be entered on the day. The proceeds of an Exemption Show must be given to a charity and are sometimes held in conjunction with small agricultural shows. Limited Shows are also available in small number, but entry is restricted to members of the club which hosts the show, although one can usually join the club when making an entry.

Before you actually step into the ring, you would be well advised to sit back and observe the judge's ring procedure. If it is your first time in the ring, do not be over-anxious and run to the front of the line. It is much better to stand back and study how the exhibitor in front of you is performing. The judge asks each

handler to 'stand' the dog, hopefully showing the dog off to his best advantage. The judge will observe the dog from a distance and from different angles, approach the dog, check his teeth, overall structure, alertness and muscle tone, as well as consider how well the dog 'conforms' to the standard. Most importantly,

the judge will have the exhibitor move the dog around the ring in some pattern that he or she should specify (another advantage to not going first, but always listen since some judges change their directions, and the judge is always right!) Finally the judge will give the dog one last look before moving on to the next exhibitor.

Gaiting the Irish Setter in the ring exhibits the dog's proper structure to the judge. The Irish Setter's gait must be free flowing and show perfect co-ordination.

If you are not in the top three at your first show, do not be discouraged. Be patient and consistent and you may eventually find yourself in the winning lineup. Remember that the winners were once in your shoes and have devoted many hours and much money to earn the placement. If you find that your dog is losing every time and never getting a nod, it may be time to consider a different dog sport or just enjoy your Irish Setter as a pet.

WORKING TRIALS
Working trials can be entered by any well-trained dog of any breed, not just Gundogs or Working dogs. Many dogs that earn the Kennel Club Good Citizen Dog award choose to participate in a working trial.

There are five stakes at both open and championship levels: Companion Dog (CD), Utility Dog (UD), Working Dog (WD), Tracking Dog (TD), and Patrol Dog (PD). As in conformation shows, dogs compete against a standard and if the dog reaches the qualifying mark, it obtains a certificate. Divided into groups, each exercise must be achieved 70 percent in order to qualify. If the dog achieves 80 percent in the open level, it receives a Certificate of Merit (COM), in the championship level, it receives a Qualifying Certifi-cate. At the CD stake, dogs must participate in four groups: Control, Stay, Agility and Search (Retrieve and Nosework). At the next three levels, UD, WD and TD, there are only three groups: Control, Agility and Nosework.

Agility consists of three jumps: a vertical scale up a wall of planks; a clear jump over a basic hurdle with a removable top bar; and a long jump across angled planks.

To earn the UD, WD and TD, dogs must track approximately one-half mile for articles laid from one-half hour to three hours ago. Tracks consist of turns and legs, and fresh ground is used for each participant.

The fifth stake, PD, involves teaching manwork, which is not recommended for every breed.

FIELD TRIALS AND WORKING TESTS

Working tests are frequently used to prepare dogs for field trials, the purpose of which is to heighten the instincts and natural abilities of gundogs. Live game is not used in working tests. Unlike field trials, working tests do not count toward a dog's record at The Kennel Club, though the same judges often oversee working tests. Field trials began in England in 1947 and are only moderately popular amongst dog folk. Whilst breeders of Working and Gundog breeds concern

151

An effortless performance in agility by a well-trained Irish Setter. Believe it or not, this is Ripley owned by handler Kristin Kamholz. Agility is great fun and exercise for dog and handler alike.

themselves with the field abilities of their dogs, there is considerably less interest in field trials than dog shows. In order for dogs to become full champions, certain breeds, including Irish Setters, must qualify in the field as well. Upon gaining three CCs in the show ring, the dog is designated a Show Champion (Sh Ch). The title Champion (Ch) requires that the dog gain an award at a field trial, be a 'special qualifier' at a field trial or pass a 'special show dog qualifier' judged by a field trial judge on a shooting day.

DID YOU KNOW?
There are 329 breeds recognised by the FCI, and each breed is considered to be 'owned' by a specific country. Each breed standard is a cooperative effort between the breed's country and the FCI's Standards and Scientific Commissions. Judges use these official breed standards at shows held in FCI member countries. One of the functions of the FCI is to update and translate the breed standards into French, English, Spanish and German.

Weaving like an expert, Poppy is losing no speed on the weave poles. Handler, Kim Holmes.

AGILITY TRIALS

Agility trials began in the United Kingdom in 1977 and have since spread around the world, especially to the United States, where the sport enjoys strong popularity. The handler directs his dog over an obstacle course that includes jumps (such as those used in the working trials), as well as tyres, the dog walk, weave poles, pipe tunnels, collapsed tunnels, etc. The Kennel Club requires that dogs not be trained for agility until they are 12 months old. This dog sport proves to be great fun for dog and owner, and interested owners should join a training club that has obstacles and experienced agility handlers who can introduce you and your dog to the 'ropes' (and tyres, tunnels and so on).

DID YOU KNOW?

FCI-recognised breeds are divided into ten Groups:

Group 1: Sheepdogs and Cattle-dogs (except Swiss Cattledogs)
Group 2: Pinschers and Schnau-zers, Molossians, Swiss Mountain Dogs and Swiss Cattledogs
Group 3: Terriers
Group 4: Dachshunds
Group 5: Spitz- and primitive-type dogs
Group 6: Scenthounds and related breeds
Group 7: Pointing dogs
Group 8: Retrievers, Flushing dogs and Water dogs
Group 9: Companion and Toy dogs
Group 10: Sighthounds

153

Practice and concentration pay off when the judge notices how professional you and your young Irish Setter appear.

FÉDÉRATION CYNOLOGIQUE INTERNATIONALE

Established in 1911, the Fédération Cynologique Internationale (FCI) represents the 'world kennel club.' This international body brings uniformity to the breeding, judging and showing of purebred dogs. Although the FCI originally included only four European nations: France, Holland, Austria and Belgium

Hannah flies over the bar jump at an agility trial. Handler, Marge Beebe.

(which remains its headquarters), the organisation today embraces nations on six continents and recognises well over 300 breeds of purebred dog. There are three titles attainable through the FCI: the International Champion, which is the most prestigious; the International Beauty Champion, which is based on aptitude certificates in different countries; and the International Trial Champion, which is based on achievement in obedience trials in different countries. Exhibitors from around the world can participate in these impressive canine spectacles, the largest of which is the World Dog Show, hosted in a different country each year. FCI sponsors both national and international shows. The hosting country determines the judging system and breed standards are always based on the breed's country of origin.

The Kennel Club's Junior Handler programme encourages young people to become involved with the sport of purebred dogs. Showing dogs is both educational and great fun, especially for responsible young people.

155

INDEX

My Irish Setter

PUT YOUR PUPPY'S FIRST PICTURE HERE

Dog's Name _____

Date _____ Photographer _____